The
FRESH
ANOINTING

The FRESH ANOINTING

MONA JOHNIAN

BRIDGE PUBLISHING
South Plainfield, NJ

The Fresh Anointing by Mona Johnian
ISBN 0-88270-668-3
Library of Congress Catalog Card Number Pending
Copyright © 1994 by Mona Johnian

Published by:
Bridge Publishing Inc.
2500 Hamilton Blvd.
South Plainfield, NJ 07080

There are occasions on which God, as it were, comes forth from his hiding place and shows to men that he is a living God, that he is still on the throne of the universe, and that he is sufficient for all of man's problems.

Henry Thiessen
(*Lectures in Systematic Theology,*
p.11, Wm. B. Eerdmans Publishing Co.)

Contents

Foreword ix
Preface xi

1. What Does It Mean? 1
2. Laughter 11
3. Joy 23
4. The Anointing 37
5. Christianity—Natural or Supernatural 51
6. Decently and In Order 59
7. Putting Your Hand to the Plow 71
8. Signs of His Coming 81
9. Shout 93
10. Key to Revival 101
11. Revival Fires That
       Keep Burning (Entering In) 109

Appendix: An Interview with Bill Ligon 127

Foreword

No matter how hard you try or how good your intentions are, revival cannot be taught, it can only be caught. Revival cannot be made to happen. It is born of a deep desire to know God, to seek his face, and to humble yourself before Him.

Revival begins with being saturated by an uncontrollable joy which then produces a fearless faith. In *The Fresh Anointing,* you will take a journey through the Scriptures, demonstrating in very practical ways that the only way to be "...strong in the Lord and in the power of His might" is to have God's joy, which is our strength (Nehemiah 8:10).

But what is the purpose of joy, or, as I like to ask, what is the bottom line? Well, that is the most fulfilling part.

Just read and see for yourself.

Richard Roberts

ix

Preface

As of this writing, the Christian Teaching and Worship Center is entering into its seventh month of revival. In evaluating this revival's brief history, we realize that the first few weeks of the visitation were crucial. Most of our people were truly baffled by the direction of the revival and hesitant to enter into anything so new. A few left the church, a few jumped in with both feet.

It was a time when a fainthearted leader would have fainted! A good report went out—a bad report went out. We were "in revival" according to one report—we were "radical and off track" according to others.

It was a time when my husband Paul and I, as founders of the church, cried out to God as never before. By His grace, we were convinced that God had begun initiating revival worldwide and we should press in whether we understood what was happening or not. We also believed that any person or church that wavered could be eliminated. In fact we have already heard of several such casualties where the anointing lasted a few weeks and then died. We did not want to miss out!

Therefore, we allowed our church to be moved along by the winds of the Holy Spirit, just as He moved in the Genesis account of creation: ...*The Spirit of God moved upon the face of the waters* (Gen. 1:2 KJV). We allowed our church to be moved as Peter described the giving of the Scriptures: ...*Men moved by the Holy Spirit spoke from God* (2 Pet. 1:21 NAS). We allowed our church to be moved as Paul was "driven along" by the force of the wind in a stormy sea.

According to Dr. William Baker, to be "moved" or "driven along" by the Spirit of God means "to be impelled by God's Spirit, fully conscious and active, steering the ship within the limits allowed by the wind." Fully aware of the risks, Pastor Paul and I made the decision to let our present program drop and sail forth with the winds of the Spirit— *fully conscious and actively participating*—steering our ship within the limits allowed by the Spirit.

By nature, culture and lifelong training, Paul and I were two who had been taught to always maintain a certain formality. It was expected of us to be "in control" and we required it of ourselves. Paul, a former concert violinist, and I, as an artist and writer, had always taken pride in our social refinement and appropriate behavior. But when we saw the revival in our church begin to waver after a few weeks, we became drastic enough to allow God to define "appropriate behavior" himself! We said, "Lord, do whatever you want with us. We'll become fools for your sake if you will continue to bless us with your glorious presence."

We could see the dramatic changes in our lives as well as in the lives of the others who "entered in" to the anointing. We did not want to go back to the desert. Our church enjoys a solid reputation for Bible teaching and for twelve years we had been trying to "teach" our people into a revival. But the strongest of Bible teaching alone had not brought the breakthrough we needed to impact our city.

When revival came to our church, in total abandonment to God during worship, Pastor Paul and I began to fall out under the power of the Spirit in front of our congregation. On several occasions I broke out in the joy of the Lord and laughed unashamedly. We leaped and shouted when the

Spirit "moved" upon us. We lost all fear of man and what others might think of us, and we continually encouraged whoever was present to enter into the same liberties. Boldly we made it clear that we were going "all the way" with this awakening!

We wanted not only our church, but all of New England, to experience another "Great Awakening." We vowed before God to do whatever it took to encourage such a move.

The early Church in Jerusalem was birthed in power through apostolic preaching and lay witnesses set aflame by the baptism of the Holy Spirit. However, within three hundred years the official Church was totally dominated by the clergy, and the laymen became religious subjects. The Scriptures were off limits for the average believer. Stripped of the Word, the Spirit and personal witness, laymen left spiritual matters to the clergy while they built a secular world.

Except for that faithful remnant God always has in every generation, only the clergy prayed, only the clergy studied the Scriptures and only the clergy gave witness of an omnipotent God who seemed far removed from the average believer. The believer's duty was to observe and obey the clergy.

According to the Apostle Paul, the ordained ministries of apostle, prophet, evangelist, pastor and teacher were given for the purpose of ...*equipping of the saints for the work of the ministry*... (Eph. 4:12 NKJV). Instead of fulfilling their scriptural purposes and preparing the saints for world evangelization, the hierarchy of the Church has frequently discouraged the saints' zeal to be bona fide witnesses of the Gospel.

The Puritans who set sail for America with a hunger for religious freedom were rigid, liturgical and oppressed laity. God used their hunger to begin a move that would one day release the whole Church body—laymen as well as clergy—to go out in the zeal of the Holy Spirit to witness in *demonstration of power and of the Holy Spirit.*

In the mid-1700s under the preaching of Jonathan

Edwards and George Whitefield, a colleague of the Wesleys, revival fires invaded the Puritan fathers of New England and blazed a new evangelistic zeal into the laymen that propelled America into the role of worldwide evangelization for the next 200 years. At a point when the Church had become apathetic to the Word, and the pulpits were filled with deistic intellectuals who stood between the Church body and any personal interaction with God, the Spirit was poured out and "strange things" began to happen. According to the writings of Jonathan Edwards and others, people went into trances, saw visions, and fell out under the power of the Spirit. It was reported that during a sermon in Lyme, Connecticut, people were so touched that their knees "smote one against the other" and strong men fell to the floor as if struck by a cannon ball. Enthusiasm, sudden conversions without class instruction stunned the clergy. Laymen began to preach spontaneously under "impulse" of the Holy Spirit. Itinerant preaching was birthed.

The "Great Awakening" in America was great! The great revivals of America set the Church free to become witnesses. The Charismatic outpouring of the seventies helped to restore the power of the Holy Spirit to the Church. And now, this present "fresh anointing" is serving to equip the saints with signs and wonders.

Six months have gone by and all wavering has subsided in our church. The evidence that continues to roll in has assured us more than ever that God is indeed pouring out a fresh anointing upon His people. "Strange things" have invaded our services with amazing intensity. Confirmed healings, deliverance from various emotional and mental oppressions, dreams, visions of the holiness of God, repentance, salvation and unparalleled worship. In fact, all of these things have come in waves, giving us a greater understanding of the meaning of the phrase "waves of revival." In any given service we are receiving three to four mighty waves of the Holy Spirit's outpouring. His presence comes in a specific way and then subsides, only to be followed by another manifestation.

I believe we are entering into a period of great conflict in the heavenlies, and God is presently equipping His people for great victories over the incoming flood of the enemy. God is equipping the saints for the next outpouring which will include massive salvations in the world. History will doubtless record the last half of the twentieth century this way:

- 1970s - early 1980s: A worldwide, interdenominational renewal, when the baptism of the Holy Spirit restored spiritual power to the Church.
- 1990s (first half): Fresh anointing poured out to equip the saints for the work of the ministry with giftings of "signs and wonders."
- 1990s (latter half): Harvest in the world.
- 2000 AD: The glory of God demonstrated upon the earth.

God has sent a fresh anointing of the Holy Spirit to revive and refresh the Church. Pastors, evangelists and individuals who want revival today can experience it. You, my friend, may have to put some effort into finding the flow, but it is happening and it can be found!

1

What Does It Mean?

Silence settled in over our congregation. It was a living silence, yet no one spoke a word. Our guest speaker, former seminary teacher and pastor-author Bill Ligon, came across the stage and sat down on its edge. Five minutes or so of waiting passed, and then Bill began walking deliberately down the center aisle. As he stopped by each person in the aisle chairs, they began to fall to the floor in laughter. Moving in a very low-keyed and unemotional manner, Bill lightly touched some of the people on the forehead and said, "In the name of Jesus."

No one was physically coerced to do anything. But before long, others picked up the joyful sound and soon the whole church resounded with a wonderful happiness. This was our fifth week of an increasing phenomena of "unusual" supernatural happenings.

"Emotionalism" and Christianity

Any Christian movement that contained even a hint of emotion has had a rocky relationship with the Church establishment for most of the past 2,000 years, but this was not always so. Our Jewish spiritual forefathers rushed to dance and rejoice with instruments and singing, to rock back and forth in fervent prayers with all their might and to fall on their faces before God. The Church today has regressed quite far from its beginnings which were birthed among those people whose greatest commandment read:

> Hear, O Israel: The Lord our God, the Lord is one! You shall love the Lord your God with all your *heart,* with all your soul, and with all your *might* (Deut. 6:4, 5 NKJV).

In this verse, the heart represents the mind, will and emotions of a person—the very center of his or her being.. The soul represents the individual's spirit. When one loves with all his heart and soul and might, he loves with eagerness, fervency and a passionate expression of feelings.

Clearly, what God is saying here is that relationship with Him should include our whole being—our bodies, our intellect, our will, our emotions, our spirit—our total ability to feel and respond passionately and publicly. Somehow the early New Testament Church chose to move away from such joyous surrender to an almighty God and began instead to wed Greek philosophy to the Scriptures, birthing a worship controlled by the mind. Tertullian of the early Church wrote:

> What indeed had Athens to do with Jerusalem? What concord is there between the Academy and the Church?.. Away with all attempts to produce a mottled Christianity of Stoic, Platonic, and dialectic composition! (*Evangelical Dictionary of Theology,* p. 444)

Why didn't the traditional Jewish freedom of emotional involvement with God continue to flow in the New Testament Church? Because the Church began to replace its Jewish roots of worship with the intellectual influence of the pagan philosophers of the day—philosophers like the Gnostics who considered knowledge supreme and the Stoics who regarded emotion as "defective judgment."

Superimpose these two worldly philosophies alone (there were several in the New Testament Church's day) over the emotional Jewish worship of God found in the Scriptures, and you get a sad mixture of religious Christianity contaminated with intellectual, snobbish leaven. This has produced a Church that often encourages a mentally-organized, emotionally-muted worship experience that recites prayers and sings songs to God as though He were a ticket holder to our performances!

Most of those in the Church who have assumed that Christian emotional expression is the result of defective judgment do not, oddly enough, usually consider tears to be unacceptable behavior. Silent tears are actually viewed as very holy—suggesting that people who know God fully have more reason to cry than to rejoice. This is not true. Joy is the expected outcome and final result of all of the experiences of God's people—including those that temporarily produce tears.

If you will search the Word of God you will clearly see that God himself moves in a full range of emotional expression just as His creation, man, does. Man's ability to express himself with broad-spectrum passion and feeling is the heart of success in life. Who wants a passionless marriage? A sports stadium of seventy thousand silent fans? A celebration with no laughter? Music with no feeling? A church filled with predictable, computer-like beings?

Definition Problem

I think we have a problem with our definition of the word "emotion." Emotion has come to mean a *state of mind.* But I believe a more accurate definition would describe emotion as *an ability to express the feelings* of the body, the mind or the spirit. Emotion is a God-given vehicle that enables us to relate to others (and God) with vibrant intensity and effectiveness. How can the Church express itself to God with all its heart, soul and might with voices that cannot be passionately raised in praise, with hands that cannot clap delightedly, with feet that cannot joyfully dance? Clearly it cannot.

3

A joyous Church cannot celebrate without expressing its feelings. This explains how many in this generation who have been taught that it is not spiritual to be emotional have arrived at a concept of public worship that resembles a memorial service. Public worship is meant to be a joyful celebration of redeemed people filled with the energizing Spirit of the living God. The Psalmist wrote:

> Make a joyful noise unto the Lord, all ye lands. Serve the Lord with gladness: come before his presence with singing (Ps. 100:1, 2 KJV).

That joyful noise unto the Lord is to come from all people in all lands! At every level of society, people everywhere are to be full and spilling over with the expression of joy unto the Lord. And they are to especially express this joy gladly in the house of God when they gather to worship in His Presence.

People throughout the body of Christ are praying for revival in these last days. I fear most of the Church today would be quite offended by the manner and ministry of God's Spirit in the mighty spiritual revivals of history. Unorthodox and unannounced moves of God always confound the human mind, overriding our well-built walls of acceptable religious behavior. True revival completely ignores the Church's struggle to maintain a reputation of respectability and decorum!

Christians today are making the same mistakes as Christians of the past—they seek an acceptable reputation in the world. But the truth is, every time the Church gets its foot inside the door of worldly "respectability," God sends revival fires that quickly convert positive publicity to persecution when the world and the religious scream, "Emotionalism! Emotionalism!" Tradition cringes at genuine revivals where men become excited, transformed and celebratory about God. The spirit of the Pharisees within the Church and the spirit of the Antichrist outside its walls will always work together to try to extinguish the zeal of people set aflame by the Spirit who takes His signals only from the Father.

The Source of Revival

True spiritual refreshings from God are not comfortable. They are painful because they demand change. A sovereign move of God that brings revival is the most unnatural thing that can occur on this earth. Not only does revival come in unannounced, but no flight plan is sent in advance whereby the men in the control tower (secular or ecclesiastical) can tell it where to land and how to behave. When God begins to move among men, He obeys no one inside the Church or out.

At some of the worst times in history, when the world has appeared to be at rock bottom, God has breathed new life into His people and great spiritual refreshings have gathered people out of every tongue and culture, and some very unorthodox things have occurred.

During the Great Awakening of the 1700s, when the Church in young America had become apathetic and demoralized by legalistic leaders who had no personal relationship with God, a fierce critic named Charles Chauncy wrote a seething review of the Church's revival meetings. He said that the houses of worship were filled day and night for a week at a time and:

> ...Unheard of instances of supposed religion were carried on...praying...exhorting (Author's note: It was unheard of in that day that laymen should pray and exhort others)...clapping their hands...laughing...crying... shrieking... roaring out; and so invincibly set were they...it was a vain thing to argue with them, to shew them the indecency of such behavior... (*Quenching The Spirit,* William D. DeArteaga, p. 51).

Charles Chauncy went on to establish the Unitarian Church in New England which denies the divinity of Jesus

Christ. Yet so persuasive was Mr. Chauncy, he managed to play a major role in stopping the Great Awakening.

Is revival, as many maintain, the result of prayer? Men do pray fervently in desperate times. But we must never attribute great spiritual moves to the desires of men and not to God. It is highly arrogant to believe that man perceives need for revival better than God so that he has to wake up God through prayer and motivate Him to action! Perhaps we would not be so surprised at the way God moves in times of revival if we did not think we ourselves had given birth to it through our prayers.

Prayer and preaching make room for revival—but they do not initiate it. The refreshings of the Lord are birthed first in God's heart and then they move downward into praying hearts that have made room for Him. The move of the Spirit that brings revival is prompted by God who only takes counsel from His own will.

Revival Has Come

Revival has come to the Church! A time of refreshment in the presence of the Lord is here now. This is a move conceived of the Holy Spirit and it is being conducted by Him as God desires. Some things about it confound the intellect. Some things excite the emotions. All things about it are giving great glory to God and lives are being dramatically altered.

Some will try to build dams and hold the waters back, denying the presence of a divine move. Some will become reckless and, seeing this supernatural outpouring as an opportunity for human success, they will drown in their own wrong motives. Others will stand aside and observe until the flow has passed them by. But many will eagerly, joyfully, passionately, recognize the presence of the Divine One in their midst and they will taste new realms of glory!

I appreciate the tedious work of good theologians who love and protect the details surrounding the Word of God.

But revivals are not birthed in scholarship any more than they are birthed in good Bible teaching alone. More often than not, revival tends to trample some of our most scholarly interpretations. But God-given revival never tramples the Scriptures!

If the Scriptures can be satisfied with this present revival in the Church, will you be satisfied? That is the purpose of this book. I want to walk with you into the heart of an outpouring of joy and demonstrations of power that the Church has not experienced for many years. It may be that no one has ever seen it quite like this. In light of the new millennium just ahead, we could be taking a drink of the great outpouring of the closing days of this age.

Is emotion involved? Yes, gloriously so! Where God's Spirit is moving, nothing escapes His wonderful touch—including man's emotions. The whole person is being wonderfully touched and caught up into the refreshing flow He is pouring out.

Why all the laughter? What is all the joy about? People falling? Claims of spiritual and physical healings? Salvations? Addictions leaving? People forgiving and embracing? What is the meaning of all this?

Only one thing is for certain—when a true Sovereign passes through, all flesh is brought low. Only things that belong to God are exalted.

Who Is On the Lord's Side?

According to the Wuest translation of Acts 2, when the day of Pentecost was fully come, there came:

> An echoing sound out of heaven as of a wind born along violently...And all were controlled by the holy Spirit and began to be uttering words in languages different from their own...Not in words of everyday speech but in words belonging to dignified and elevated discourses.

Then Peter stood up and quoted Joel, saying:

> And it shall come to pass in the last days, saith God, I will pour out of my Spirit on all flesh: and your sons and daughters shall prophesy, and your young men shall see visions, and your old men shall dream dreams. And I will shew wonders in heaven above, and signs in the earth beneath... (Acts 2:17,19 KJV).

There is a generation where life is not going to continue in its ordinary pattern, spiritually speaking. People of this generation will continue to work, marry, buy and sell, but spiritual forces on the earth will be released upon mankind and a great dividing line will be drawn. Just as Moses drew his line in the sand, the question will be: *Who is on the Lord's side?*

Those who join the side of God's foes today will find supernatural ability to enjoy unprecedented lewdness and sacrilege. Wealth will run through rebel fingers like water, and ungodliness will actually make more sense to them than righteousness. On the other hand, those who choose to stand on the Lord's side will also taste the supernatural powers of another world.

Multiple Moves Coming

Signs and wonders—events that defy ordinary explanation—are slated for the last generation that will flow with the moves of God. There will be multiple moves, just as the waves of an ocean roll in one upon another. I believe those in the closing days of this age will see the glory of God rolling in with one outpouring after another. Signs and wonders are already beginning to appear in the congregation of believers.

Weigh the facts if you must. We certainly did. Investigate for yourself, but do not be alarmed at the demonstrations and manifestations of God's renewing power in the Church. This manifestation must precede the return of the Lord. Signs and wonders are heralds of His coming.

Judgment on the ungodly and revival among the people of God—two entirely separate entities—have often walked parallel through history. The Church must learn to identify itself as a separate entity from the nation in which it is located. Regardless of the moral or political position of any nation's government in these last days, the people of God within that system can draw waters from the wells of salvation.

The Return of the Rope and Bucket

As a child growing up in rural America, my family had a well with a long rope attached to a bucket. The water was deep in the earth, pure and refreshing. But in order for our thirst to be quenched, we had to unwind the rope, drop the bucket into the well and pull it to the surface.

For the past ten years or more, the Church has seemed to lose its rope and bucket. Our zeal has faded, our witness in the marketplace has greatly diminished. Sin and setbacks in the Church, combined with the major advances of spiritual skepticism in the world, and the Church has been drying up. But God is restoring the rope and bucket! Isaiah prophesied long ago:

> Therefore with joy will you draw water from the wells of salvation. And in that day you will say: "Praise the Lord, call upon His name; declare His deeds among the peoples, make mention that His name is exalted. Sing to the Lord, for He has done excellent things; this is known in all the earth. Cry out and shout, O inhabitant of Zion, for great is the Holy One of Israel in your midst!" (Isa. 12:3-6 NKJV).

A new outpouring of joy from the Presence of the Holy One of Israel is being released upon the Church! It is a sign that is going to shake the nations. For those who are thirsty, it is going to be a time of divine satisfaction and the harvest will be great and divergent. The awakening that is beginning now among the people of God is going to branch off in numerous directions, but each stream will ultimately converge with other anointings until the Anointed One himself appears.

These are the last days and God is pouring out His Spirit on all flesh. Demonstrations of God, signs and wonders, are slated for the heavens and the earth. What does it mean? The Church is being equipped to flow with the Spirit of God for a great harvest. Surely it will be the Church's finest hour.

There has never been a time quite like this. There has never been such opportunity. Like a magnificent aircraft, we are becoming "airborne" and there is no turning back!

2

Laughter

I received a phone call from my brother just as I was leaving for our Monday evening service. "I know you're on your way to church," he said, "but my grandson (Author's note: A handsome, sixteen-year-old young man from a wealthy, nominally Christian family) just left and I thought you would want to hear what happened to him yesterday. You understand more about 'this' than we do."

"This" was in reference to the revival coming upon the Church today. As yet, the Methodist and Baptist churches my brother and his grandson attend have not experienced this fresh anointing. Their only exposure has been what they have heard from our church twelve hundred miles away.

My brother began his story, "Last night, Madison was with his girlfriend at the Baptist church when he broke out in uncontrollable laughter! He laughed and cried and rejoiced all the way home. When he got there, he went in and woke up his parents and nearly scared them to death. They thought he must have had an accident. Then Madison came to see me today to tell me about it."

"I don't care what my peers think," Madison told his grandfather. "I don't care what anybody thinks. I just want to be alone with Jesus."

Paradox in Motion

Nothing describes this present time better than to say we are a generation of increasing momentum. We are paradox in motion. At breakneck speed, both good and evil systems of thought are pelting the human race with new and outlandish rapidity. For example, to many people today the life of a whale or a spotted owl is just as sacred (if not more so) as the life of an unborn human being. Such a conclusion leads one to believe that true value judgments have been bred out of many in this generation.

The life span of almost every new idea fades—some in one year, some in a season or a day—in the light of something alluringly "newer." Things are under production right now in industry and technology that are already out of date. Rising and falling "stars" fill the daily news as fortunes and reputations are being built and swept away overnight.

Multiple fads are overlapping each other until no one can say what is "in" at any given moment. On one hand, individuality has been enthroned as the ultimate accomplishment. On the other hand, group identification has engendered legalized "causes" that range from worthy to worthless.

The world's systems are failing, and they deserve to fail as arrogance and natural wit are their foundations. As Nobel prize winner Elie Wiesel said of unfaithful Samson, "People who end up blind and imprisoned were blind and imprisoned long before they got there." But in the face of all the chaos, God is doing an amazing thing in the Church. A supernatural fire and joy have invaded our struggling programs and walls of every sort are tumbling down.

Divine Invasion

Both my husband Paul and I are the product of the 1970s revival that swept through the Church—Protestant, Catholic and Orthodox—birthing millions into the Kingdom of God.

Paul, then a violinist and professor of the string department at a leading university, was totally consumed with classical music when the revival of the seventies touched down in our university town. At that time, I had been seriously ill for two· years and was looking for a miracle. I not only received my miracle, but Paul was born again, along with our son and daughter and their families. Within five years, we were all in full-time ministry and began establishing a growing, healthy church in Boston, Massachusetts.

There was a totally supernatural, divine invasion of our family that has never slowed down. For the past fifteen years, we have still faced numerous problems—but we have traveled hundreds of thousands of miles in more than twenty nations, ministering the Word of God. We have experienced many wonderful things.

At the direction of God, I have given myself to concentrated study of the Scriptures, privately and at the college level. I have devoted every possible moment to writing, producing more than thirty books and booklets which have been translated and published in numerous languages. We have prayed for the Church universal to become effective in this generation. We have worked long and hard doing what we have believed to be God's will wherever and however we could.

But by the year 1993, Paul and I could deny it no longer. The zeal of the Church, the effectiveness of the Church worldwide, was losing its impetus. Joy and the anticipation of God's presence no longer occupied the hearts of His people.

Christian magazines and flyers filled with suggestions and the "answers" crossed our desks:

- "The next great move of God is liturgy!"
- "The Church is taking Jesus to the streets through rock and rap!"
- "Pull down strongholds over major cities through invasion rallies!"
- "Let's get an effective political agenda!"

13

Effort! Effort! Effort!

Some of what we were seeing was good effort, but Paul and I agreed that it was not a combined effort equal to the rapid growth and impact of sin and turbulence worldwide. "Nothing short of a sovereign move of God can combat the challenges we face today," we admitted to each other. "Lord, unless You move, nothing any of us do will overturn this generation's headlong rush towards disaster!"

This became our prayer as well as our lament. We understood that our world had gone beyond the control of man. Only God himself was equal to the task of bringing the chaos into control.

Nothing But a Sovereign Move

Had I been God looking in upon the arrogance and irreligious behavior of modern society, what would I have chosen to do at such a time? With the carnality and murmurings of a world-infested Church, had I been God I would have sent a veritable blast of spiritual fireworks capable of creating a celestial choir out of one-celled amoebas! Had I been God, I would have at least thundered forth from heaven with words that would have disemboweled a generation impacted with self-admiration.

But what did God do? He sent a supernatural joy and fire upon the Church that has people rolling in the aisles. Amazing!

Paul and I just shook our heads as we watched our longtime, trusted friends and pastors fall to the floor with laughter one night at a very "spiritual" banquet. "What on earth are they doing?" we asked each other in confusion. "This is God?" Hundreds of otherwise dignified, composed people had just finished dinner one evening when a minister among us got up to speak and suddenly laughter broke out over the room. People began to gently fall onto the floor and lie there as though they were basking on the beach. We were stunned, amazed and flooded with ques-tioning. "How could this be God?"

Salvation Birthed in Joy

Why indeed would the Creator from whom all creation has issued pour out joy and laughter for the healing of such a sick generation? Simple. The plan of redemption itself was birthed in laughter.

After the fall in the Garden of Eden, man needed redemption. Step one in the outworking of this divine plan came when God called Abraham out from the world of paganism in order to follow Him. Abraham was seventy-five years old when God told him to go to a far country where He would make of him a great nation, numbering his seed with the very stars themselves.

Abraham obeyed, but many years passed and still no heir was born to fulfill this prophecy. In desperation Abraham and his barren wife Sarah devised a scheme for an heir through a surrogate mother and a son named Ishmael was born to him. Trouble, not redemption, was born of Abraham and Sarah's effort to fulfill God's plans. All human effort apart from God is fruitless and eventually counterproductive. Another thirteen years went by until:

> And God said unto Abraham, As for Sarai thy wife...I will bless her, and give thee a son also of her...she shall be a mother of nations; kings of people shall be of her. Then Abraham fell upon his face, and laughed... (Gen. 17:15-17 KJV).

Approximately one year from Abraham's laughter (at the age of ninety), barren Sarah bore a son and, according to God's instruction, they named him "Laughter!" Isaac means laughter. *And Sarah said, "God has made me laugh, so that all who hear will laugh with me"* (Gen. 21:6-7 NKJV).

15

> And God said to Abraham, ...*In Isaac* [meaning laughter] *shall thy seed be called* (Gen. 21:12 KJV).

Has the Church heard this today? Heard what? That the Redeemer came from Isaac! Yes, we have heard, and now here we are—four thousand years later—laughing the laughter of Sarah. God put that joy and laughter into Sarah's soul. On the day Isaac was born, a joyful laughter went up from the household of Abraham to God. It was the same joy-producing laughter that has been released in every generation since.

> When the Lord turned again the captivity of Zion, we were like them that dream. Then was our mouth filled with laughter, and our tongue with singing: then said they among the heathen [nations], The Lord has done great things for them (Ps. 126:1,2 KJV).

Laughter from God has power in it to transform lives and circumstances, and people of all nations take note when God so moves. Lives and circumstances change and liberty and blessing result. The Church becomes visible to the unsaved when God stirs it with laughter. God himself even laughs!

> He that sitteth in the heavens shall laugh...thou, O lord, shalt laugh at them; thou shalt have all the heathen in derision (Ps. 2:4; 59:8 KJV).

Do you have the God-view of your circumstances and your fears? If you do, then you have cause for laughter. Laughter is an expression of joy according to Webster's dictionary. Who should be bubbling over with joy more than the redeemed people of God, those whose redemption was birthed in joy and laughter? Jesus confirmed as much when He said:

> Your father Abraham rejoiced [jumped for joy] to see my day: and he saw [perceived by the Spirit] it, and was glad (John 8:56 KJV).

16

Abraham jumped for joy over the plan of salvation that the Holy Spirit unfolded before his eyes.

Divine Joy

It was divine joy the lame man experienced when Peter spoke the name of Jesus and set his ankles free from crippling weakness. He went *walking, and leaping and praising God.* It is the same joy you and I are supposed to express when we are persecuted:

> Blessed are you when men hate you, and when they exclude you and insult you and reject your name as evil, because of the Son of Man. Rejoice in that day and leap for joy...! (Luke 6:22, 23 NIV).

It is the same joy that filled a yet-unborn babe and caused him to leap in Elizabeth's womb. People who argue that unborn babies are not people should get the God-view of this issue. God's Word settles the question: When does a baby become a person? At conception, a soul is set in motion. And by the sixth month, that baby can be filled with the Holy Spirit, perhaps before.

When Gabriel came from the presence of the Lord to tell Mary that she would bear Jesus, he told her that her cousin Elizabeth was also pregnant in her sixth month (see Luke 1:36). Shortly thereafter, Mary went to visit her cousin. As soon as they saw each other, look at what happened:

> And Mary arose in those days, and went into the hill country with haste, into a city of Judah; and entered into the house of Zacharias, and saluted Elisabeth. And it came to pass, that, when Elisabeth heard the salutation of Mary, the babe leaped in her womb; and Elisabeth was filled with the Holy Ghost (Luke 1:39-41 KJV).

John the Baptist was filled with the Holy Spirit at his sixth month of conception. He "jumped for joy" with

17

rejoicing at the presence of Jesus who was just beginning to develop in Mary's womb. Listen now to the Holy Spirit's declaration through Elizabeth:

> And she spake out with a loud voice, and said, Blessed art thou among women, and blessed is the fruit of thy womb. And whence is this to me [granted to me], that the mother of my Lord should come to me? For, lo, as soon as the voice of thy salutation sounded in mine ears, the babe leaped in my womb for joy (Luke 1:42-44 KJV).

Divine joy energizes the entire human body, mind, emotions and spirit. It is God's will that His joy totally consume our whole being all the days of our natural life. Only as we are thus consumed are we able to fulfill our purpose in carrying out the commission to go into the nations with the Good News of the coming King.

A New Momentum

A new momentum has come into the world in these days. Demons have been loosed from Sheol. "Dante's beasts" have initiated a sophisticated army of lust and pride that the Church is incapable of overcoming on its own. The wealth, the intellectual stockpile and the sheer manpower being poured into evil systems is mind boggling. Pornography, demonized toys, pagan visualization in education and psychiatry and base sensualities are being funded today by unimaginable wealth. But all of it combined cannot compare to a Church that is funded by the fire of the Holy God.

The Holy Spirit has been sent from God to set His people free to leap and rejoice in His great salvation in spite of the state of this world. The method by which God operates is His choice—the power is His, the glory is His. We have only to enter in and receive.

Many stories will be related in the ensuing pages that show the impact this fresh anointing is having on the lives of individuals. But here I would like to relate the miracle of Cindy, a victory story that I consider to be one of the greatest to come out of this revival.

The Miracle of Cindy

We met Cindy about twelve years ago. Bubbly and vivacious, she was among our first converts in Boston. Over the years her husband became a deacon and one of the pillars of the church. But shortly after Cindy committed her life to the Lord, she went into a tormenting depression, and for the past ten years, she had been slowly sinking into a physical and emotional wasteland. Her bright blue eyes and infectious laughter turned to bitter reprisals which regular psychiatric and pastoral counseling seemed unable to touch.

By her own admission, Cindy was tormented and tormenting to those who loved her. Many times she sat in Pastor Paul's office on the verge of giving up. Her sturdy frame literally became skin and bones. "She is not going to make it, short of a miracle," we finally conceded. When she managed to attend Sunday morning services, Cindy sat languishing as though she would simply die of weakness right before our eyes.

When the revival came to our church, Cindy made three small, but significant, steps toward her healing:

1. She began to attend the services more regularly.
2. She agreed to work a few hours a week in the church office to get out of the house.
3. She committed to taking a Bible course at the Kaleo Bible Institute located on our church grounds.

One Thursday evening, the telephone rang at our home. I overheard Pastor Paul saying, "Cindy, that's wonderful! Praise God, that's just wonderful!" When he hung up the phone, Paul turned to me and said, "Mona, God has touched Cindy tonight. I mean she *has been* touched!"

But how much God had touched Cindy, we had no idea. For five days Cindy stayed under the anointing of the Holy Spirit. When she came to church she began praising God in a loud voice, and every hair stood up on our bodies! It was like the voice of Lazarus calling from the grave. Cindy stood and spoke with the voice of an evangelist. She was emaciated, a skeleton of a person, but we all wept and rejoiced at the same time as she walked the aisles praising God.

So great is the anointing on Cindy that the people she touches fall to the floor under the power of God. So restored is her soul that she is a walking voice of strength and power. The moment her counselor saw her after the visitation, she said, "What has happened to you, Cindy? Something has happened. Your whole face is changed!"

And so it is. Cindy has been resurrected from an emotional grave that held her in bondage for ten years! To God be the glory!

Renewed Love

Speaking in broad-spectrum generalities, I would say our church is now experiencing the supernatural blessing of God that we had never been able to bring about through our countless hours of well-intentioned brainstorming. God did in moments, through the vehicle of spontaneous joyous laughter, what all of our concentrated efforts had never seemed to get off the ground.

A renewed love for God and for each other has come over our people. Tolerance for each other's differences, a desire to be helpful, eagerness to be together has flowed into our midst. A heightened awareness of our fellow human beings has suddenly come to life within us. To see people simply "caring" for someone else in a fast paced, multi-ethnic, major city like ours is truly a miracle in itself. All our hearts are undergoing a transformation from stone to flesh. We are celebrating a love feast in the house of God!

As one member said, "I no longer simply tolerate people, I actually care about them!"

The blessings are not only spiritual and emotional, they are coming in physical healings, too. A call came in to Pastor Paul one day that one of our members had a blood clot on his lungs. He was not only in serious condition, but hospitalization and recovery would be extensive. Since a close friend had died with the same condition one week before, we knew the gravity of the situation. Pastor Paul prayed and two deacons from our congregation were sent into Boston to anoint our brother with oil. That was on Monday. By Saturday, the man was released from the hospital with a clean bill of health and came to church to give testimony. Laughter and celebration resounded as we heard him declare, "Our God is God!"

One young mother in our midst who was expecting her fourth child was burdened, unhappy, depressed and bitter. Her attentive husband found her attitude beyond his help. After observing the revival in our church for several weeks, Kathy entered in through the door of laughter and was totally revived.

> I was dead, unforgiving and bitter. During a recent service I fell to the floor under the power of the Holy Spirit, and while I was lying before the Lord, a joy and peace began to well up in my heart and wash away all my deadness. Happiness has returned to my life.
>
> This is not only a happiness during the worship services! My husband and I have developed a special worship time together where the joy of the Lord often visits and we laugh and enjoy His presence in our home!

And that is not all. Come with me now to see what else a fresh anointing from God produces.

3

Joy

Joy has always been the chief desire of man. Joy, to some, comes under various labels such as "achievement," "satisfaction," "fulfillment," "fun/pleasure," or "happiness." But, regardless of the label of choice, the entire human race wants a happy, satisfying life. Even the Constitution speaks of the pursuit of happiness as an inalienable right of man in America!

Rich or poor, the need for joy even supersedes our drive for power. Men want wealth because it gives them power. They want power because they think it will make them happy. They believe that happiness will finally satisfy the internal gnawing within them for fulfillment. They are half-right. Joy will fulfill them, but wealth and power can neither buy nor take over "joy." Jesus alone brings true joy into a sorrowing, hungry heart. He has clearly said that His joy is the key to our satisfaction:

> Until now you have asked nothing in My name. Ask, and you will receive, that your joy may be full (John 16:24 NKJV).

Dante's Beasts

In the early fourteenth century, a political writer named Dante wrote a three-part work called *The Divine Comedy.* The theme of this work was Dante's search for the "Mountain of Joy." In order to find this desired mountain, he had to confront three beasts:

1) The leopard of malice and fraud.
2) The lion of violence and ambition.
3) The she-wolf of incontinence.

These same "beasts" form the framework for the major systems of thought that control and distress today's society:

1) **Malice**—the desire to do evil to another.
   Fraud—deception and lying to others for personal gain.
2) **Violence**—unnatural disregard and abuse of others.
   Ambition—the desire to excel beyond others.
3) **Incontinence**—lack of self-control in relation to others.

I do not believe that man's inhumanity to man has ever been more depraved on a worldwide scale than it is in these last days. Human life has become expendable on busy metropolitan streets, small town street corners and along roadsides throughout our own nation. Men, women, young people and children are the daily victims of man's desire to do evil to another for personal gain and a seemingly total lack of self-control in relation to others.

We live in a day when demonic forces are gaining unprecedented access to governments, educational systems, the pleasure industry and the media on a global scale. For the sake of power, pleasure and publicity, natural man will do almost anything—and he has. But nothing seems to have made him happy, for this is by and large a miserable

24

generation. And what should we expect? A world that looks only to itself gets only itself for a solution.

In the world, this is to be expected—but what about the Church? Aren't we supposed to be a different kind of people? Yes—we are to be unique in our contrast to the rest of the world. We are to be like a light shining in a dark place!

The Body of Christ has a rich, spiritual inheritance which it is fully entitled to draw upon and then show forth as a light upon a hill. But it never will unless its members grow up. The Apostle Paul said that an heir, so long as he is a child, is no better off than a servant *though he be lord of all.* Those in the body of Christ who refuse to move beyond being as "a child" will continue to live as servants in darkness, bondage and sorrow—with no more power and answers than the world!

The Source of the Power of Joy

The things of God often seem very strange to the natural mind, even to those of us who have been walking with Him for decades. I clearly remember the day Paul and I walked into a meeting where a man with a South African accent was pacing back and forth like a professional football player on the side lines of a play-off game. As he said, "Be filled with the joy of the Lord," joyous laughter erupted all over the vast auditorium. Raising our brows in surprise, we looked at each other with questions in our eyes.

Without hype or any apparent provocation, Rodney Howard-Browne was calmly, but joyfully, flowing in an undeniably supernatural power. Uniquely joyous laughter and physical manifestations seemed to be springing forth everywhere we looked. Paul and I knew we had to determine the source of this power and then respond accordingly.

This is precisely what I began to do the moment the wheels of our jet plane touched down, returning us to Logan Airport in Boston. After six days of continual meetings where I had watched senior citizens, business executives, housewives, college youth, even children, break out in uncontrollable laughter—or tears—or a catatonic muteness, I rushed to the Word in search of understanding. I very much needed to compare these happenings with recorded outpourings of God's Spirit at other times in divine history.

I took my Bible, used with caution for forty-two years, along with numerous theological works and I began to research the word "joy." How often we refer to "the joy of the Lord." But what does this actually mean, I asked myself? The Word says that "a merry heart does good like a medicine." But what does this actually mean?

I knew that there are different kinds of medicines. One kind goes into the body where it fights against sickness and disease. Another kind of medicine, tranquilizers for example, does not fight a virus or a germ, rather it is designed to give one a sense of well-being. Nothing is actually cured and nothing changes but one's outlook, and that is usually quite short-lived.

Does God's joy simply make us "feel" better until it wears off? Or does His joy cause an actual healing, curative action upon our bodies, minds and situations that brings about change? This is what I had to find out.

Joy Defined

According to several of my favorite sources, such as Colin Brown and *Kittle's Theological Dictionary,* three basic words define joy in the original Greek:

Chairo: Physical well-being as the basis for joy.
Euphraino: Subjective (self-reflective) feelings of joy.
Agalliaomai: Outward demonstrations of joy in public worship.

Joy can be described as literal well-being, both physical and emotional. But joy is also the outward expression of this well-being in demonstrations during public worship. Because the Church has largely limited joy to an "inward sense of well-being with God," we have never really experienced its genuine power as a *medicine* for our souls.

Having been in ministry for sixteen years, and being married to a pastor, I feel confident in saying that many Christians are unhappy. We deal with them regularly. They are unhappy, in spite of their peace with God, because their soul is infected by the spirit of the world.

These people are crusty, defensive and inflexible. Their minds, wills and emotions have yet to be invaded by the attitude-changing Spirit of God. Joy is one of God's "invading agents" that penetrates the self-protecting attitudes we have built around our lives to let healing into our relationships, our souls and our bodies. Joy makes a way, by penetrating the crustiness, for the healing to come into sorrow and pain. Joy causes us to open ourselves up to new possibilities. Even the world knows that laughter has disarmed many potential disasters and can often break through uncomfortable walls of disagreement and stalemate.

The Church simply has not placed much value on the benefits of joy's supernatural power to spiritually heal because it does not understand how it works. It "works" in somewhat the same way an antibiotic "works." An antibiotic can do its work, invading and overwhelming that which has impaired our physical body, even when we do not understand its actual method of operation. Do all who take a prescribed antibiotic know exactly what is happening when they take it, or do they take it because they have faith in their doctor?

At the point in my life when I was both physically and emotionally ill (mentioned earlier), I learned to "take" expressive worship—singing, clapping my hands and dancing—before I took my prescribed medicine. My spiritual medicine set my soul free, which greatly affected my physical condition as well. Entering into joyful worship is a medicine prescribed by the Greatest Physician. Joy is a gift from God that fights for us, and through us for the sake of others, as surely as natural medicine fights infection.

This is what is happening in this fresh rain of joy we see spreading throughout the Church today. God is equipping individual believers with healing power that will allow each one to go out into a sick and hurting world with the "antidote" for sickness and need. Joy is power—*divine, supernatural, energizing power*—imparted to us through the anointing of the Holy Spirit.

Jesus himself was anointed with joy. It was only through *the joy that was set before Him* that Jesus endured the cross (see Heb. 12:2.). Joy's power strengthened Him to face His impending death. Joy allows the mind to circumvent the senses so that we are able to see our circumstances from a bigger, spiritual picture, while fear focuses and freezes the senses on the moment. How this awesome power flows out of joy, I cannot fully explain. I only know that since our church has come into this fresh baptism of joy, we have lost our fear.

Without exception, the testimonies are repeatedly the same, "I just don't care what others think!" This certainly does not mean that we have become negligent—just the opposite. We care about everything that is important more than we ever did before. We are appreciative, grateful, concerned—but fear of negative opinion has been greatly diminished in our lives. Somehow, faith that God is clearly at work overshadows everything else. Joy releases us from the present limitations of our most pressing circumstances to step into the realm of faith and spiritual possibilities.

Joy is spiritual; it is literal; it is physical; it is emotional and unless it is somehow circumvented, joy invariably insists upon becoming public! Human beings may suffer in silence, but no one ever keeps joy to himself or herself. When our cup begins to personally "overflow," joy is written all over us. Joy is a public witness and attraction to nearly everyone who comes in contact with it. The Church in Jerusalem grew because they fellowshiped *with gladness and singleness of heart, praising God...* (Acts 2:46,47 KJV).

Possession of the Whole Person

For a minute, let us go back in time. The Greek word for joy, *agalliaomai* (meaning the outward demonstration of joy in public worship) had very interesting usage in its original secular setting. In the pre-Christian world, joy meant to adorn, plume oneself, make a show, boast of something, enjoy, experience pleasure, be in raptures (ecstasy). Joy described an experience which took *possession of the whole person!*

When Jesus exhorted the Church to ask in His name that our joy would *be full,* He knew that full divine joy would totally consume the person. Jesus knew that a man full of joy would be like a peacock in full plume, boasting of the beauty of God adorning his life. God longs to make a show of His glory through a Church caught up in "ecstasies of joy." In these present days of "canned laughter," God wants a people who will display deep, genuine happiness that will spill over the walls of the Church and bubble out into the market place.

How popular do you think any major sport would be if every seat in the giant coliseums were removed and the games were played in total silence? Entire sports leagues would become impoverished. Worship services that make no room for the joy of the Lord to be received and expressed, impoverish those participating.

Do some people get carried off into extremes when joy's emotional flow is released? Obviously, some do. But this is no excuse for the Church to go running back into the safety of its "proper and acceptable" traditional behavior!

According to records of the first "awakening" to hit the colonists of New England in 1734, it is painfully evident that quenching the Spirit of God is a dangerous proposition. Jonathan Edwards, the scholarly Yale pastor, was enjoying two years of great revival when he began to be pressured by Boston pastors to rebuke some laymen who had taken it upon themselves to pray for other laypersons. This was something only the pastors were permitted to do. When he caved in and did so, the revival died. Edwards tried to re-spark the move of revival, but was unfruitful until George Whitefield came from England with a fire that totally ignored the negative opinions of the clergy.

I believe Pentecost sent a message to the Church that says God is more interested in sparking empowered zeal than enforcing rigid religious rule. The Holy Spirit, who has charge of the Church, has the necessary power to control any human-created "wild fires" that might erupt.

Jesus said His believers were to be like "lights" and "cities set on a hill." In other words, Christians are to be the public access channels for the demonstrations of God. Any time we try to be otherwise, we fall into the same error as Israel. A major point of contention between God and His ancient people was their continual drawing back from their mandate to be a spiritual light to the nations.

God wants witnesses of His truth. Did you know that one of God's titles is "famous"? He wants to be known far and wide. We are to be His bright lights, His open books and His anointed mouth pieces. The Church is to arise and shine that all may see. Faith's joy and beauty are meant to flow out of us in public expression.

Private faith is a myth perpetuated by man!

Yet, it is not by any works of our flesh that we bring forth this witness. God has not asked us to save, heal or deliver anyone. He asks only that we be a vessel out of which His anointing can be poured to save, heal and deliver. Why? To prepare the earth for His return!

To Gethsemane with Joy

On His way to the Garden of Gethsemane, Jesus made some final statements to His disciples. This was to be His last opportunity to equip these men who were about to face soul-shaking events. What did He say? What truths were vital to these men who were about to experience the crucifixion

30

of their Master and receive fearful threats upon their own lives?

To begin with, Jesus reassured them that He was the "True Vine," and He told them that all branches that would have eternal life must live in obedient fellowship with the Vine. Jesus then said to them:

> These things have I spoken unto you, that my joy might remain in you, and that your joy might be full (John 15:11 KJV).

He was saying: "Remember who I am and draw from my joy and my strength into yourself like branches naturally draw from their vine." Through the parable of the vine and the branches, He was preparing them for the way the power of the Holy Spirit would continually release joy into their lives. On the way to His own arrest, trial and death, Jesus revealed joy as a key to overcoming all opposition.

When it is rightly understood, what better weapon for overcoming a present tragedy than a real surge of empowering joy? In a few hours the disciples would see Him crucified on the dreaded Roman cross. This would call for fresh power in the lives of those who were seemingly "left behind." Knowing this, Jesus gave them not an arsenal of weapons or a hiding place—but He gave them His joy to remain in them that their joy might be full. This was not a little sprinkling, nor a tiny stream Jesus spoke to them about, but it was to be a river of joy that would fill them. This river of joy would overflow their natural limitations and send them out into a pagan world—fearless and unstoppable.

Spiritual Equipping

I believe this present outpouring of joy upon the Church is in fact an equipping of the Christians to overcome their natural limitations and the deceptions and persecutions that are multiplying in these last days. Signs and wonders, and power and great joy go hand in hand.

Luke records in chapters five and six of Acts that ...*by the hands of the apostles were many signs and wonders*

31

wrought among the people... (Acts 5:12 KJV), and that a young deacon named Stephen who was *...full of faith and power, did great wonders and signs among the people* (Acts 6:8 NKJV). Then in chapter eight, Luke said that:

> ...The people with one accord gave heed unto those things which Philip spake, hearing and seeing the miracles which he did. For unclean spirits, crying with loud voice, came out of many that were possessed with them: and many taken with palsies, and that were lame, were healed. *And there was great joy in that city.* (Acts 8:6-8 KJV, italics mine).

This kind of joy did not go unopposed. These same believers came under great persecution and rejection. But what did they do with their rejections? When Paul and Barnabas were expelled from Antioch, they *...shook off the dust of their feet against them* and *were filled with joy, and with the Holy Ghost* (Acts 13:51,52 KJV). About rejection and fiery trials, Peter said:

> Beloved, think it not strange concerning the fiery trial which is to try you, as though some strange thing happened unto you: But rejoice, inasmuch as ye are partakers of Christ's sufferings; that, when his glory shall be revealed, ye may be glad with exceeding joy (1 Pet. 4:12,13 KJV).

These early Christians learned firsthand that great spiritual advances always evoke great spiritual conflicts—but God is always in control. Something the current body in the Church has often failed to remember is the fact that the events of these last days—no matter how evil—are never outside the control of God. Satan has not, does not and is not going to roam anywhere on this earth to do anything that escapes the Creator. God's power only intensifies in expression when evil threatens to engulf the world.

Intensified Power Impartation

God's outpouring of supernatural joy is the means of imparting that intensified divine power to the Christian for great spiritual works in these darkening final days! The more joy you have, the more power. The more power you have, the more fruit your life will bear for God's honor.

From this fresh outpouring upon the Church, the anointing is flowing into people through the power of the joy and laughter. Every infilling is life changing. Depression is leaving people. Addictions are being broken. Holiness is being sought after. Relationships are being healed. Forgiveness is flowing among enemies. Just sitting in the services where the anointing is present is bringing more power into those who are hungry for more of Jesus.

A young father who was unknown to anyone in our church came into one service. "I was so depressed I could hardly function," he admitted later. "But as I sat in the service, the depression left me and I feel like a totally different person!" How was this possible? It was the power of God's supernatural joy flowing within the service!

Some of my greatest moments of joy come as I fellowship with the Lord around His Word. Sometimes I walk around my home or office, clapping my hands with joy over some glimpse of truth the Lord has shared with me. Life is a wonderful discovery that is meant to be enjoyed fully. Life is a far more worthy celebration than a concert performance or an Olympic contest.

As Jesus continued on His way to Gethsemane, He kept equipping His disciples for the difficult days that lay ahead of them. He was imparting divine power to them through the gift of His joy. He explained that He would be leaving them soon, saying to them:

> ...I will see you again, and your heart shall rejoice, and your joy no man taketh from you (John 16:22 KJV).

33

As a Christian, it is possible to be filled with a joy that is not subject to the natural environment or its circumstances. That is because true joy has no source or basis in the natural. I know a mother who became so filled with the joy of the Lord at her young son's funeral that she laughed in the Spirit in place of mourning in her soul. Psychology has an explanation for such a reaction, but the Scriptures' explanation is older. Did not Jesus raise the widow's son from the dead and turn her tears to laughter? Perhaps Jesus gave my young friend a glimpse of that same resurrection.

I watched a pastor who had gone through a life-shattering experience stand to address a conference of ministers, but the Holy Spirit had joy awaiting him at the podium and not one intelligible word ever came out of his mouth. The joy of the Lord came upon that middle-aged, well-dressed man and he laughed for the next hour. Even after the meeting continued with another speaker, the man sat down and continued laughing. I saw that same man the next day and he was as calmly ordinary as anyone you might meet.

Another pastor stood to address a gathering of approximately fifteen hundred people. He had just returned from Russia with a glorious report of the move of God there. Before he stood to speak, joy filled the auditorium and laughter bubbled over everywhere. Not having been in this outpouring of the Spirit prior to that evening, the minister took his Bible and proceeded to speak. The only problem was, he could not find his text from the book of Joshua. He looked and looked, but he simply could not locate it. Closing his Bible, the minister smiled and said, "What God is doing here is greater than what I have experienced." And he sat down.

With no previous experience of this new manifestation, this man of God knew even though he did not understand what was happening, it was of God. I was impressed with his spiritual sensitivity that recognized God's hand in something that many have deemed disorderly. Deep within myself, I heard these words, *If you will enter into this present move of God, you must be willing to adjust your programs on the spot.*

34

Holy Spirit Order

"Decently and in order! We must do things decently and in order. The Bible itself commands it," cry those who are frightened by that which is beyond traditional "order." Unfortunately, today's definition of "order" in the Church often means pre-organized and intellectually-controlled spiritual activity. I know all about that kind of "activity," for I am a champion organizer and clock watcher. But as I have observed the flow of services bathed in this new outpouring, I see complete order. How amazing! The only things that have changed are the method and the one in charge.

Under the leadership of a pastor submitted to the Holy Spirit, God makes room for all things—spiritual worship, the teaching of His Word and the ministry of the Holy Spirit. The full experience of God and the full release of His blessings become manifest as the Holy Spirit directs.

The early Church was directed by the Holy Spirit. Jesus sent Him for just that purpose. How is it that man has become afraid to relinquish control to the very Spirit who enables us to do anything of a spiritual nature in the first place?

True spiritual hunger has caused men and women to pursue every avenue imaginable within the framework of traditional spirituality to bring God's Presence back into the Church. God has seen our attempts to make our services attractive to Him so He would desire to manifest His Presence in our midst. He knows that the hunger and the longing for Him is beginning to override the fear of being "improper" in our services.

So what does He do? He pours out laughter upon His people. Surely it is clear to those who critique "such things" that laughter is not a humanly-mandated, proper program for today's Church in the light of all the criticism it has suffered. But it is God's program and it's more powerful than all of man's programs put together.

Joy's Credentials

Spiritual joy is forging new breakthroughs in the Church today. And is it any wonder? Look at joy's credentials:

Joy overcomes trials: *...Count it all joy when you fall into divers temptations* (James 1:2 KJV).

Joy overcomes persecution: *...Greatly rejoice, though now for a season, if need be, ye are in heaviness through manifold temptations* (1 Pet. 1:6 KJV).

Joy overcomes suffering: *They departed...the council, rejoicing that they were counted worthy to suffer shame for his name* (Acts 5:41 KJV).

Joy has an eye for the future: *...When his glory shall be revealed, ye may be glad also with exceeding joy* (1 Pet. 4:13 KJV).

Joy maintains itself in affliction: *I am exceeding joyful in all our tribulation* (2 Cor. 7:4 KJV).

Joy is an everlasting promise: *Therefore the redeemed of the Lord shall return, and come with singing unto Zion; and everlasting joy shall be upon their heads: they shall obtain gladness and joy; and sorrow and mourning shall flee away* (Isa. 51:11 KJV).

Joy is heavenly: *...Joy shall be in heaven over one sinner that repenteth* (Luke 15:7 KJV).

The Scriptures tell us that the Apostle Paul finished his life's work with joy (Acts 20:24). His prayer for the Church was that we might be filled with all *...peace and joy in the Holy Ghost* (Rom. 14:17 KJV).

All "...joy in the Holy Ghost" *is* being poured out upon the Church today. It is an anointing for which millions the world over hunger to experience.

4

The Anointing

Deep calleth unto deep, said the psalmist (see Ps. 42:7). One of the purposes of a "fresh anointing" from God is to stir up, to *calleth up,* the anointing that lives within every believer. ...*The anointing which you have received of Him abides in you* (1 John 2:27 NKJV), but from time to time, it needs reviving.

A fresh anointing has come upon the Church and good things are happening! God is working in very real ways in the lives of His people today. Both spiritual and natural changes are taking place.

The title of this book is The Fresh Anointing. What does that mean? For months now, as we sing in our services, we sense the manifested presence of the Holy Spirit in our midst. Many times during the week we have gone into the sanctuary and sensed the Presence of the Holy Spirit. One young man cut through our sanctuary on the way to kitchen recently. He came out stunned, saying, "Boy, I felt the presence of God in there!" What does this mean?

"Anointing" is a powerful word in the Old Testament that many believers have little understanding of today. Even though we call our Lord "Christ" in the New Testament, which means "anointed," I believe that the average Christian sees little direct bearing of this word on his or her personal life. Why?

Anointing Defined

The ancient use of the word anoint simply meant to rub in or smear on oil. Quite often it was a fragrant oil. The Old Testament use of this word among God's people signified a transfer of authority, power and honor. By pouring oil upon God's priests or His chosen kings, these individuals became spiritually empowered to conduct the business of that office.

King Cyrus of Persia had not received the sacrament of the anointing oil as had the kings of Israel when the term "anointed" was extended to him by God. Thus, anointed came to mean a person chosen for a special commission, but totally dependent on God and His plans.

We might say an anointing is three things:

1) Being recognized by God.
2) A transfer of authority, power and honor from God.
3) It may include a specific commission from God.

Several years ago I did a series of teachings on the subject of the anointing. The best definition I could come up with was this: The anointing is the power of God coming upon a life for God's purposes and God's glory.

Certainly to anoint one is a biblical event which represents a literal transfer of divine power here on earth. It is a transfer of power which God uses men to pass on to one another.

Early Church Anointing

When Jesus sent out His twelve disciples to minister, Mark records that:

> ...They cast out many devils, and anointed with oil many that were sick, and healed them (Mark 6:13 KJV).

Anointing was definitely a part of the early Church beliefs and practices. James said:

> Is anyone among you sick? Let him call for the elders of the church, and let them pray over him, anointing him with oil in the name of the Lord. And the prayer of faith will save the sick, and the Lord will raise him up. And if he has committed sins, he will be forgiven (James 5:14-15 NKJV).

Obviously the olive oil within itself had no curing power for the healing of diseases. But the command to anoint one with oil in the name of Jesus, praying and believing Him to touch that person, was a blessing that promised *transferred power!* The use of oil was employed, no doubt, to remind us that it is not by man's *might, nor by power, but by my Spirit,* that God heals people. Oil in the Scriptures is representative of the Holy Spirit. What a sacred privilege to be a vessel of transferred anointing!

This blessing was passed on to the Church just as it had been given to Israel. The power of God is transferred when anointing takes place in His name with faith. It is a ministry that applies to any believer who will exercise obedient faith.

Anointing Today

On stage at a conference, Rodney Howard-Browne, Bill Ligon and Sid Roth were standing beside my husband Paul when he had just finished playing his violin. Rodney walked over and laid hands on him, praying for a fresh anointing to touch him. Paul felt no particular sensation at the time, yet when we returned to our church the same unique manifestations that had occurred at the conference began happening in our congregation. People fell to the floor when Pastor Paul laid hands on them. Laughter and joy began to bubble up all over the congregation. Tears began to fall and stony hearts began to soften.

From that day until now, the same things have been occurring in our services. There was definitely power given through this fresh anointing which had been transferred by faith and the laying on of hands. I received a letter recently from a "Christian Adventist" who had attended one of my services at a conference in New Hampshire:

> When I arrived home, our very next service experienced the same things that took place in your meetings. I brought ten women to that meeting with me and we will never be the same.

Such transformation is nothing new or unusual in the program of God. The Church's problem is that it has lost sight of some of its most fundamental truths such as the laying on of hands. Hebrews 6:1-2 calls the act of laying on of hands a *basic, foundational doctrine* of the Church.

Looking back some thirty-two hundred years, we find a beautiful example of what actually transpires with the laying on of hands. Israel wanted a king, so God spoke to Samuel, His judge and prophet, to anoint a young man from the tribe of Benjamin named Saul.

> Then Samuel took a vial of oil, and poured it upon his head, and kissed him, and said, Is it not because the Lord hath anointed thee...the Spirit of the Lord will come upon thee, and thou shalt prophesy...and shalt be turned into another man....
>
> And it was so, that when he had turned his back to go from Samuel, God gave him another heart...and he prophesied among them (1 Sam. 10:1,6,9,10 KJV).

The laying on of hands is one way of releasing the anointing. The anointing then releases the Spirit of God within a life. Yet it does not flow without opposition.

The Spirit Against the Anointing

Psalm 2 says the kings and rulers of the earth *take counsel together against the Lord and his anointed* (Christ). There is a spirit, an unseen power, on the earth that is set against the anointing of God. It was (and is) against God's people Israel; it was against Jesus and it is against the followers of Jesus. This hostile spirit works through ignorance of God's ways as well as through Satan-inspired, power-hungry people.

This explains why Israel is continually harassed over their sliver of a nation. Their divine mandate to maintain God's property for His Son's coming Kingdom—the Kingdom of His *Anointed* One—is a thorn in the side of Satan! The anointing of God is real, with the authority of God himself behind it. It also has all hell attempting to discredit it.

The anointing releases God's power in order that God's plans may be accomplished. Churches that resist the demonstrations of the Spirit, however unwittingly, quench the flow of the Spirit. Unwittingly or not, these churches encourage those who take counsel against *the Lord and his anointed."*

Those of the world do not understand the ways of God. Spiritual moves and outpourings are foolishness in their sight. But the world's opinion cannot hinder the flow of God within the body of Christ. Only one thing can hinder the flow of the Holy Spirit and that is the Church itself. Jesus said of His visit to Nazareth that He did not do many mighty works there because of their unbelief. He said to the Pharisees, ... *Ye made the commandment of God of none effect by your tradition* (Matt. 15:6 KJV). Could this be the reason why there are so many powerless, dry churches today? J. I. Packer thought so:

> Can we doubt that the present barrenness of the Church's life is God's judgment on us for the way in which we have dishonored the Holy Spirit? And, in that case, what

41

hope have we of its removal until we learn in our thinking and our praying and in our practice to honor the Holy Spirit? (*Knowing God,* J. I. Packer, p. 63.)

Tradition can be a killer of the flow of the Holy Spirit because man almost always resists altering his religious traditions. This resistance boils down to the question of who is in control. One of the first things God made clear to us in this divine move was that He was the only one who would control this fresh anointing. We were going to have to set aside everything we had planned. His words were: *If you will flow with what I am doing today, adjust your services and sermons to comply with My Spirit.*

Paul and I were concerned. How should we conduct our services? Should we speak first, then sing—or sing first, then speak? We decided to begin with singing and then wait for the leading of the Spirit as to how we should proceed. One thing became immediately obvious, our twenty minutes of announcements had to go! For this the congregation applauded.

Walking cautiously through our new format, we simply did our best to flow in the direction the Spirit was going. And it has worked! Until this day, we are remaining as flexible as we can. If the music extends naturally, we keep singing. If it is cut short, we move on to the message or a testimony. As a result, our services contain the same elements (with the exception of announcements) as before. The only difference is, there is more life-changing anointing. Our worship and praise has literally become two hours of basking in the presence of God with signs and miracles. The Word is then received with open arms.

Courage to Break With Tradition

D.J. Ligon and I were sitting in a service together when she reached over and drew my attention to these few but powerful words uttered to Jesus by certain Pharisees: *Why do thy disciples transgress the tradition of the elders?* (Matt. 15:2 KJV).

"Mona," D.J. said in amazement, "Jesus' disciples transgressed religious tradition!" She is right. Every fresh move of God brings a certain transgression of religious tradition. Walls of man-made ritual crack whenever the winds of God's Spirit begin to blow.

Every church service should be altered when the Presence of God manifests among us. We make exceptions for natural dignitaries, should we do less for a visitation of God? How can we be led by the Spirit and not find ourselves continually adjusting to His manifested presence?

The Church has the same problem as Israel. Israel had a religious routine and when God manifested himself visibly in the person of Jesus, He disrupted the Jews' temple ritual. Jesus manifested in the flesh, right there in their midst, demanded change. Talking about the Messiah, reading the Scriptures about the Messiah was no problem to them. The conflict arose when the Messiah actually appeared!

The Church has no problem *singing about* the Holy Spirit, the joy of the Lord and the fire of His Presence. But when the Holy Spirit manifests and overpowers people and they fall to the floor, or joy breaks out in laughter and celebration, or people are healed—then the oppressing spirit that worked in the Pharisees quickly sets to work in the Church. If it is not withstood, the works of the Lord among us are quenched.

This book is an effort to withstand opposition to this new awakening in the Church. From the moment hands were laid on me and I entered into the fresh anointing, I have had a burning in my soul to write and encourage both ministers and laymen to open their hearts and minds to this new refreshing from the presence of God.

There is power, joy, energy and anticipation in the manifested anointing of God. Yet, this does not mean every person in that Presence will be touched and commissioned. Nor can we predict where He will manifest His Presence next. By His Sovereign will, God decides when, where and upon whom He will pour out fresh anointing.

43

Our church is also involved with the present outpouring of God's Spirit on the former Communist world. On a recent visit there, I saw that no person has to work to bring revival to that part of the world. All one has to do is jump in and flow. The Spirit is moving there abundantly. Praise God, the same is happening in the Church around the world. A call came in recently from Norway. "We have heard about your revival. Will you come over? We want the best first!" Revival is the best.

Do All Get Touched?

The manifested Presence of the Holy Spirit is moving in the United States of America once again. Everyone who is hungry for more of God, who will press in to touch God, will be blessed. Since this is a sovereign move, some who are not aggressively seeking God's flow will be swept in, but others standing on the outside may be left "on the outside." Many Christians resist moving in as they say, "If God wants me to have something, He will give it to me." This is not necessarily true. Energy must be invested in anything of value. Nothing "just happens."

The Scriptures say that all who hunger will be filled. Some who are not hungry may also be brought into experiencing this fresh anointing—others may not. God is not dictated to by anything other than His own will, and He has only promised to fill those who hunger. He has instructed us to seek, to ask and to knock—to express our hunger. Those who do so will be filled. Those who don't may or may not. Can you afford to take the chance? Whenever God is pouring out His Spirit, every saint should actively seek a fresh infilling. Personally, Paul and I are still drinking and seeking for more.

An interesting story of one who was not actively seeking to join in involves a Boston policeman who was convicted of a felony and sentenced to one year in a correctional institution. During his incarceration, Paul and I visited with him on several occasions. After his release he began attending our church and has been a regular member since. When the fresh anointing came to our church, however, this former policeman was very skeptical, saying, "Whoa, I don't know about this. I just can't see it." He consequently made no effort to enter in.

Recently, this same man came to me with a big smile and said, "I really didn't go for all the things that have been happening since the revival. But three months ago (when our revival began) I felt God was telling me to cut the cable wires, put away my television set and give more time to Bible study. I did and it's just great what God's been showing me. Then two weeks ago while I was taking a shower, I began to laugh so much I thought I would drown in the water. My mouth kept filling up, but I couldn't stop laughing. And it happened again on another day!

"Well, this week my sister called me and, to my total surprise, she told me that for the past few years since my conviction she has continued to pursue my pension from the police department. In spite of their initial decision to the contrary, they are restoring my pension!" As I said earlier, this fresh anointing is being manifested spiritually and naturally.

Seek, Ask and Knock

Do you want a fresh anointing? Then get into services where the anointing of God is present and enter in with all your being. Worship, sing, rejoice, pray, be sensitive to the Holy Spirit. Allow Him to flow into your life. Is your church dry and thirsty? Then you begin to become the lightening rod for the fresh anointing of God to sweep into your church. How do you do this? By seeking, asking and knocking on the door of revival. Break with tradition. If you are the pastor, invite a trusted minister who has already entered into the fresh anointing to share with you and your congregation. God will respond. Do what Paul and I did. Buy a plane ticket and investigate revival meetings.

Active worship is necessary to life-changing fellowship of the anointing of God. Already we see a trickle of pastors and church leaders coming to our Monday evening and special services, pressing in for a fresh anointing for their lives and for their churches. Word is spreading.

This move of God will eventually be everywhere so that all who are truly hungry may be filled. There is a corporate anointing that is truly awe inspiring that comes into a worship service where the people are hungry enough to accept it. The power of God literally rolls in like waves where leadership and laymen come together in unity with what God is doing at this moment. Mere words cannot describe its impact.

One recent Sunday morning, as I walked in front of the stage, the Holy Spirit said, *Lie back on the stage and wait upon me.* In front of the people, I sat down on its edge and lay back—something I would never have done before the revival. As I lay there, God gave me this word for the people: *If you want to get wet, stand under the shower. If you want to get soaked and saturated, you need to lie down in the tub. Some of you here today will be called to lay down your lives and become saturated with the things of God.* Many responded and confessed their lukewarmness in rededication. Some were slain in the spirit and lay in God's big bathtub for saturation.

It was like a reminder of Ezekiel's vision where man entered into God's stream first to the ankles, then to the knees, then to the waist and on out into the deep. God is calling the Church to plunge into the deep water!

Above all, do not allow yourself to be robbed by fear of man. Determine in your heart to follow the promptings of the Holy Spirit, regardless of any opposition of man. Flesh is always diminished in the Presence of God and the proud or those who feel their comfort zone or their sphere of influence is being threatened will not respond well to the diminishing of their flesh. If you want this fresh anointing, expect and allow your flesh to be humbled in His Holy Presence. Refuse to allow your flesh to continue conducting your life, your ministry or your church service if you are the minister in charge.

This is a time of refreshing for all who will jump in and flow!

One of our members came to me recently and said "Mona, every time I fall under the anointing of the Holy Spirit, He ministers wonderful truths to me. The Lord is making me aware of the need to give Him more time, to be more conscientious about what He gives me to do."

It was a similar refrain I had heard the day before from one of our worship leaders who said:

> My experience with God had become ordinary over the years. One day it dawned on me that I no longer had the peace and joy that had once been such a part of my daily Christian experience. My once joyful explorations of God in prayer had become obligatory. Prayer was my Christian duty.
>
> Some time ago as I watched television, a commercial ran for a movie called *The Remains of the Day.* Suddenly, the Lord spoke very clearly. "The remains of the day is just what you give to Me." I was stunned! Following that encounter I got on my knees and asked Him, "What should I do? I want my old joy back, the old peace and continuous knowledge of Your presence." As I listened, the Lord said these words, "Be led by My Spirit."
>
> God had just begun to do a wonderful work of revival in our church. The Lord was healing, restoring, delivering and revitalizing people as never before. Finally, I also experienced this refreshing to the point that I became drunk in the Spirit, through laughter and tears, during two of the services. It was an indescribable experience of God supernaturally overtaking my whole being. Once this outward manifestation was over, something deeper began to take place inside me. The Lord became precious to me once again!
>
> Since then I have entered into a realm with God that I never knew before. During personal times, I've had marvelous intercession, worship and intimacy with Him

that is on a whole new level. And one burning desire has arisen which supersedes all others—to know Him more and to obey Him even in the tiniest little things that no one else knows. His Presence has become my most precious possession.

The hungry are being restored by this fresh anointing. People who have not been in church for years are coming again. One young teenager broke down and sobbed as Pastor Paul began to tell her how much Jesus loved her and the good plan He had for her life. We learned later that this young girl, because of family objections to church attendance, had very little experience of any kind with God.

Dozens of children have fallen to the floor under the power of the Holy Spirit as hands have been laid on them. A boy of nine has had repeated visitations where God continues to assure him that he will *preach His Word.* This anointing on the children has taught us that God knows no age limit. The work is done by the Spirit to whosoever He wills.

Hardened Hearts

Do we really believe what is happening is a supernatural manifestation of God's Presence? Are we sure of what we are seeing?

The disciples were with Jesus when He supernaturally fed the five thousand. Shortly thereafter, when He walked on the water to meet them they were blown away. Mark records that ...*they were sore amazed in themselves beyond measure, and wondered* (Mark 6:51 KJV). Why did they accept one genuine supernatural manifestation and not the other? Why does the Church believe a soul can be "born again" or "born of the Spirit," but a spiritual joy or a miraculous healing cannot happen by the same divine power?

The answer lies in the next words of Mark. The disciples were puzzled because ...*they considered not the miracle of the loaves: for their heart was hardened* (Mark 6:52 KJV). They were capable of being insensitive to the miraculous in their midst because they had seen consistent demonstrations of the supernatural, and they no longer took great delight in the presence of Jesus' power. They did not discern each miracle as the Church does not discern miracles today because our hearts are caught up in things other than the Spirit.

No sooner had the revival broken out in our church than church leaders began to warn each other that the Christian Teaching and Worship Center had become radical and off-base. Some are somewhat gentler, telling us that this is nice for us, but not for them. Even though wonderful fruit is resulting and several genuine miracles have occurred, the hearts still need to be softened!

It takes time to wait on God and reverence His works among us. Before the new refreshing came, Paul and I were aware that people wanted to get in and out of church quickly. But, oh, how different it is now! How delighted we are to wait to see what God will do in each service. Sometimes we wait until midnight, and even then we do not want to leave the presence.

As the Church, let us not fear His presence, nor fail to appreciate the signs and wonders given to us by God. Not only do they have purpose far beyond our ability to understand, but they continue to remind the world that a mighty God is still revealing His glory to a people among them.

5

Christianity–Natural or Supernatural?

The world calls Christianity a religion, but how would you define it? If Christianity were a product, I think the Church would have difficulty identifying and marketing it. How would they capture its true "essence" in words that would fit within current marketing strategies?

Is Christianity a natural moral code for social sanity? If Christianity is natural, then its benefits are no more supernatural than a good set of Boy Scout rules. Is Christianity simply spiritual, a metaphysical sphere where men can hope for something beyond natural matter? If so, then its benefits are vague and its operations unidentifiable.

Is it a supernatural spiritual code offering alternative hope to a failing world system? If so, then man is confined to an endless struggle between good and evil systems. If Christianity is supernatural, however, a living organism with a divine program that is supernaturally conducted and empowered by the Spirit of the Creator of all things, then it is beyond the control of man, and we are beholden to the One who is in charge. While natural people and events are caught up in this divine program, the life that moves it forward is purely supernatural.

I understand the world's view of Christianity. They can

discredit its supernatural content because they do not believe its claims. I do not, however, understand the Church's view of Christianity that sometimes causes it to discredit the supernatural. Christianity without the supernatural is reduced to the scam of the ages built around a visionary Messiah and a myriad of false claims.

Do you know how many supernatural claims are attributed to the birth of Jesus? In Luke's account, chapter one, the announcement of His birth alone contains twenty supernatural events.

Christianity is not natural—it is an impartation of the supernatural. It is the supernatural life of Christ imparted to natural man. Nothing about this relationship between Creator and the created is natural. Christianity is the supernatural operations of God in His natural creation.

The Holy Spirit is the third Person of the eternal Godhead, with all of the ability of God the Father and Christ the Son. John declared that Jesus would baptize His followers with the Holy Spirit and fire.   The Holy Spirit still has the same power to release the fire of God on earth as He did on Mount Carmel over the altar of Elijah. One who releases supernatural fire that can instantly consume an animal sacrifice, its stone altar and the water from the trenches around it, can certainly bring about dramatic changes in the lives of human beings!

The nature of fire is to give off energy while it burns. It is one of the most powerful forces in creation. The sun, upon which all natural life on this planet depends, is a massive ball of fire. The nature of an "inflamed" Church, operating under the anointing, is to give off an energy so consuming that souls locked in fleshly addictions and weaknesses are confronted in a way they cannot escape. Under the anointing of the Holy Spirit, men will either be set free or highly offended. I believe this is one purpose of the fresh anointing we are presently experiencing—God is confronting man in a powerful, inescapable manner. The fire of the Spirit is falling.

Confrontation

After I finished speaking in one of our services, I walked toward the back of the sanctuary where two men seemed to stand out from all those around them. I knew immediately by the Holy Spirit that these two men needed a personal relationship with God. As I began to address the first young man by telling him how much the Lord loved him, he panicked. His eyes darted back and forth and I saw the urge to run written all over him.

Most people who come into a church are pleased to hear that God loves them. But not those who are running from God and certainly not this young man! Two rows away, I stopped to minister a good word to the other man the Spirit had pointed out. In a different reaction, yet just as desperate as the first man, the second gentleman flew into an anger so intense that sparks seemed to shoot out of his eyes. He demanded his coat and fled from the church, outrun only by the first man whom the Spirit of God had confronted.

Confrontation, the Holy Spirit said. *This fresh anointing is going to confront the deepest corners of men's hearts and bring forth whatever is hidden for good or evil.*

Would Jesus confront people in a crowd and put them on the spot? Is that really the way God operates? I asked myself these questions after the incident I just related. Immediately Matthew 12 came to mind.

In the New Testament, we read where a man with a withered hand was in the synagogue during a meeting when the subject of healing on the Sabbath was brought up. The tradition-bound legalists were against his being healed. Jesus, on the other hand, confronted both the subject and the man:

> And he said unto them, What man shall there be among you, that shall have one sheep, and if it fall into a pit on the sabbath day, will he not lay hold on it, and lift it out? How much then is a man better than a sheep? Wherefore it is lawful to do well on the sabbath days. Then saith he

to the man, Stretch forth thine hand. And he stretched it forth; and it was restored whole, like as the other (Matt. 12:11-13 KJV).

But what was the response of the people to Jesus' bold demonstration of His healing power? Immediately after Jesus had violated their religious tradition, their way of conducting a worship service:

Then the Pharisees went out, and held a council against him, how they might destroy him (Matt. 12:14 KJV).

A fine young pastor, hungry for more of God, came to our center. Friends warned him against this "new thing" happening in our church. He came anyway. As the service progressed, that same pastor fell to the floor in laughter. He was drunk in the spirit for more than two hours. He returned again for two other services where each time he was profoundly touched and anointed by the Spirit of God.

The next Sunday when the pastor stood to speak in his church, several members of his congregation were touched in a tangible way by the power of God. "I have never preached with such power!" he said excitedly. But his celebration was short lived. The "Pharisees" came in and said, "This does not fit the tradition of our church. We want this stopped immediately!"

The sheer gall of the Church is amazing! Without even going to God, we make our judgments as to what the Holy Spirit can and cannot do in our assembly. We act as though God has actually appointed us to be the keeper of His flame.

What If?

What if Jesus is coming soon? What if this is the season to usher in His Kingdom age? What if we are the "signs and wonders" generation? How are we going to stand in God's Presence and explain why we refused to flow with His Spirit?

54

I have constructed a hypothetical letter from the majority of the Church to God. It goes like this:

Dear God:

The problem has come up again about the fact that you used to be supernatural. Well, perhaps you still are, but we with the pure doctrine understand that you do not perform supernaturally anymore. We have the Bible. From it we read and believe all the wonderful things you used to do for those who trusted in you. At the same time we understand that we are not to make fools of ourselves by expecting you to do the same things today. That would stir up emotionalism and create confusion—not to mention division.

We have hospitals for our bodies, psychiatry for our tough emotional and mental problems, counseling and support groups for mid-week sharing of our miseries. We have well-timed, one-hour worship services—once a week—where we gather to hear about what you used to do and to keep the doctrine pure about how you did it.

Thank you for letting us know how powerful you could be if it were the right dispensation. Hope to see you one day, when it's all over.

Sincerely,

The Church Majority

Denying the Power

The Church today has created a strange religious demand. On the one hand, we demand the highest moral standard and adherence to the Word of God in all Christendom. On the other hand, we do little teaching and introduction to the mighty Holy Spirit who gives the power to live up to the demands of the Scriptures. We teach the Word with utmost intensity, yet we *deny the power thereof* of that same mighty Spirit-filled Word to enable *us* to fulfill our purposes in God.

If the Word alone were sufficient, Jesus would not have sent the Holy Spirit (see Acts 1:4-5). If the Spirit alone were sufficient, Jesus would not have given the ministry gifts to the Church: the apostles, prophets, evangelists, pastors and teachers to equip the saints for the work of the ministry (see Eph. 4:11-12). The Church is to be empowered with both the Word and the Spirit of Jesus Christ, functioning in the supernatural gifts imparted by the Spirit.

No local church, no denominational group of churches can afford to set aside either the Word or the Spirit. Jesus made it clear, *Ye do err, not knowing the scriptures, nor the power of God* (Matt. 22:29 KJV). It takes knowledge of both the Word and Spirit and an impartation of the supernatural power within both to live the maximum Christian life.

My mother is eighty-two years of age. She recently has had heart bypass surgery twice within six months. Weak and sitting on the sofa for the bigger part of the day, she said to herself one evening, "I'm not getting any stronger." She got up and turned the television channel to a series of ministries. As they prayed, she prayed. As they worshiped, she worshiped. As they praised God and quoted the Word, she praised and quoted the Word.

"Strength began to enter into my body!" my mother related. "I said, Lord, maybe it's only for one day, but at least I have strength right now. But the next day the strength was there again, and again, and again!"

Oh, for a greater awakening among God's people to cry out for what we have yet to grasp! Why do we feel that God is so pleased with our programs and rituals, that we should continue to hold on to what we have to the exclusion of anything else He has for us? So what if a shaking of our carefully constructed traditions occurs and some seem to run too fast with spiritual "manifestations"? It is much easier to stamp out a little wild fire than it is to resurrect the dead. Great moves of the Holy Spirit can survive the handful of extremists and the over zealous who always jump on for the ride. Supernatural moves of God do not create flakes or extremists. They just expose those who are inclined toward imbalance.

Let each one of us earnestly seek to enter into the new thing God is doing. There is refreshing in the Church today for all who hunger for more of the true "God life."

Not Really New

For generations, the majority of my family has been Methodist. A sainted aunt who has now gone to be with the Lord was a lifelong member of the Methodist Church—a well-meaning body of believers who were so unemotional and organized that a smile was almost out of order. Until this fresh anointing of the Holy Spirit, I had not thought of my aunt or her church for years. As I began to share this "recent outpouring" with my mother, she stopped me, "I know what you're talking about. Your aunt used to laugh until she fell back in the pew at Wesley's Chapel."

Suddenly, I recalled a scene I hardly knew still existed in my memory. As a child and then as a young teenager, I had watched a beautiful glow come upon the face of my aunt as she began to quietly laugh. With her arms folded in front of her, she would gently shake with laughter until she either sat or fell into her seat. There she would enjoy the presence of the Lord for as long as she liked.

How many in that starchy little congregation were aware of this, I do not know. But God knew. It was an unquenchable spark from the Wesley revivals that had once turned the whole world right side up.

This fresh anointing is not new. It has been tried and tested by saints who stood the test of time. During her life, my aunt had to work in the fields with her seven children and live in a tiny house with no special amenities. She had given up one son to a war and a daughter and a husband to cancer. My aunt had every reason to mourn. She chose instead to take joy and draw water from the wells of salvation. She had a Christianity that was greater than her natural circumstances.

When the anointing of the Holy Spirit came to Wesley's Chapel, even if everyone else missed Him, my aunt refused to be robbed. She entered into the joy of His Presence and laughed her way through a happy life.

6

Decently and In Order

On the day of Pentecost, power came rushing out of heaven. It was power too great to be confined to any man's printed program.

I shared the message of this chapter at a First Baptist Church in New England. Following my delivery, the congregation responded with applause and approximately twenty people were baptized in the Holy Spirit. There was one confirmed healing and scores of others with various sicknesses received prayer. Words of knowledge were ministered. At least sixty percent of the congregation fell to the floor under the power of the Holy Spirit where they lay in communion with God in tears, laughter or peaceful silence. This was certainly not "order" as usual for this dear church. Some might even call it disorderly.

It is a serious indictment to call *anything* "disorderly" that the Holy Spirit does during a worship service. Such presumption can cause even a sincere believer to walk dangerously close to blasphemy. Jesus warned:

> Anyone who speaks a word against the Son of Man, it will be forgiven him; but whoever speaks against the Holy Spirit, it will not be forgiven him, either in this age or in the age to come (Matt. 12:32 NKJV).

The Word Confirmed

We must realize that we have learned our existing "spiritual" pattern for order in the Church from centuries of the control of man. Jesus is the pattern for the Church and the Church is the pattern for the unbelievers. Look at the pattern Jesus established. Notice the amazing absence of department reports, special fund drives, announcements and so forth! His ministry on earth was essentially threefold:

1. He ministered the Word to His followers.
2. He witnessed of God to the lost.
3. He performed signs and wonders, ministering to the suffering through the gifts of the Holy Spirit.

The Church's commission and pattern is to continue the ministry of Jesus until He returns. Jesus, as the Head of the Church, set the pattern for Christian ministry:

1. Minister the Word to believers.
2. Witness to the lost.
3. Allow confirmation of the Word by signs and wonders following.

Paul verified that the ministry of the Word was to be confirmed by signs and wonders when he wrote to the church at Corinth and then again to the church at Thessalonica:

> My speech and my preaching were not with persuasive words of human wisdom, but in demonstration of the Spirit and of power (1 Cor. 2:4 NKJV).

> Our gospel came not unto you in word only, but also in power, and in the Holy Ghost... (1 Thess. 1:5 KJV).

Decently and In Order

Paul also made it clear to the believers at Corinth to:

> Let all things be done decently and in order (1 Cor. 14:40 KJV).

The Greek word for decently, *eushemosune,* means well formed. The Greek word for order, *taxis,* means in an orderly manner with official dignity. So, even the most joyous of worship services are to be conducted in a well-formed, dignified and orderly manner.

I can almost hear the words of the response following the collective sigh of relief from many "proper" believers: "We *always* knew this disorderly behavior of Pentecostals was unscriptural!" But before we jump to such doctrinal conclusions, let us be open to see the whole scriptural portrait for "orderly" public assembly.

The Apostle Paul's address regarding manifestations (the spiritual gifts) of the Holy Spirit during public worship was not, by any stretch of the imagination, intended to silence the demonstrations of the Spirit. To put something in order does not mean to eliminate it. If Paul's intention had been to eliminate spiritual gifts in public worship, he would have said, "Let all manifestations of the Spirit cease!"

What Paul said instead was, *Follow after charity* [love], *and desire spiritual gifts, but rather that ye may prophesy* (1 Cor. 14:1 KJV). Following this Spirit-breathed statement, Paul then lays some ground rules for the operation of spiritual manifestations beginning with their purpose to build up the Church in the ongoing ministry pattern of Jesus Christ.

The New Testament, as far as I am able to determine, records only one kind of church service—one that clearly had spiritual manifestations present. The Books of Romans, Acts, Corinthians and Thessalonians all refer to such spiritual demonstrations.

Spiritual manifestations (demonstrations) of the Holy

61

Spirit build up the body of Christ. They do not simply "boost its morale," as some would contend. They do not stir up the people into an emotional frenzy, as others would rush to point out. Demonstrations of the Holy Spirit during a worship service build the Church in the same way an architect perceives the act of building from a blueprint on his drawing board. This is what the word edify means—to build as an architect.

The Church's problem lies in the fact that it has lost its image of the Architect. Because we have violated the Second Commandment, we have created an image of God and Christ as mortal. We no longer know the indescribable God of Moses at the burning bush. We no longer know the Christ who appeared to John in the Revelation.

Taking a typical painting of the "gentle" Christ, I placed it before a congregation one evening. Then I read John's description of what He actually looks like. The congregation was stunned at how much we have compromised Christ's image.

What image do you perceive when you think of Jesus? How does it compare with John's description? John said of Jesus that He was

> ...clothed with a garment down to the foot, and girt about the paps [chest] with a golden girdle. His head and his hairs were white like wool, as white as snow; and his eyes were as a flame of fire; And his feet like unto fine brass, as if they burned in a furnace; and his voice as the sound of many waters...and his countenance was as the sun shineth in his strength (Rev. 1:13-16 KJV).

The strength of our glorious Lord Jesus is like the sun at high noon! What can't He do for those who love and trust in Him—to those who have the Spirit's image?

The church at Corinth was not wrong to move with the power of God. What they needed was instruction in how to move more effectively. Their participation in the supernatural manifestations simply needed regulating.

Manifestations of the Spirit

In chapter 12, Paul makes it clear that the gifts of the Holy Spirit are supernatural abilities of the Holy Spirit. Spiritual gifts cannot be "learned," nor are they the product of the natural abilities of spiritually sincere believers. Please note that the Apostle Paul calls these gifts the *manifestations of the Spirit.* He does not call them inspirational expressions of spiritual men (see 1 Cor. 12:7.)

The second thing Paul reveals is the fact that the supernatural gifts of the Holy Spirit are "given to every man" so that the Holy Spirit may manifest himself through all people in the Church. The gifts are not meant to be manifested through a select few, leaving the majority out.

The power belongs to Jesus The commission belongs to the followers of Jesus—all those who believe. On the day of Pentecost, when the Holy Spirit fell, He fell on all who were present in the upper room. The fire tongue of God set upon each of them. They all spoke in tongues and all came pouring out of the upper room giving witness.

To the natural eye, it would appear that "people" are prophesying, healing, giving tongues and interpretation, performing miracles. Such is not the case. Supernatural manifestations of the Holy Spirit are initiated and performed by the Spirit as the Spirit wills—the believers are merely the vessels. We might naturally liken spiritual believers to transformers that are capable of conducting spiritual "electricity" from God to others. We transmit into manifestation that which the Spirit of God initiates: Word of wisdom, word of knowledge, faith, healings, working of miracles, prophecy, discerning of spirits, tongues and the interpretation of tongues (see 1 Cor. 12:7-10).

These gifts are of the Spirit, under the full control of the Spirit, and they are manifested only as He wills. No man can initiate a manifestation, nor can man select what gifts will manifest. While we do have a part to play in flowing with the move of God, we cannot "make" the gifts happen. We have only to be sensitive and willing to allow them to happen through us.

Traditionally, what the Church calls an "orderly worship service" is a humanly planned and controlled service where the Holy Spirit is allowed to minister only silently. In these services, the Holy Spirit is generally not allowed to manifest himself with any of His gifts and public demonstrations except the new birth.

Public manifestations of the Holy Spirit are termed "out of order" by a large part of Christianity. This excludes Pentecostal and Charismatic services to some extent. We have learned, however, from our present revival that not all Charismatic churches are open to this new outpouring from God. Many pastors we expected to rush toward the revival are actually distancing themselves publicly for the time being.

If quiet and controlled worship were preferred by God, then why did He make such a noisy, fiery display of the arrival of the Holy Spirit? Why didn't those one hundred and twenty people walk quietly out of the upper room, with their hands artistically folded in prayer, whispering praises to God? The Spirit himself was as noisy as a mighty, rushing wind about His coming. The upper room He came into was shaken and filled with tongues of fire!

The Purpose of Worship

Believers are to assemble together in a church service primarily for three purposes, which are covered by Paul in his first letter to the Corinthians, chapters 12-14:

1) To minister to God in praises and worship.
2) To receive the Word and ministry of the Holy Spirit's gifts for the edifying—building up—of the believers.
3) To serve as a witness to the lost who may be present.

64

Worship is a spiritual encounter. The Holy Spirit is always present whenever believers gather together to empower the people to praise and worship God, to anoint the minister to teach or preach the Word, to hear and answer prayer, and to convict of sin. He is also present to confirm the Word "with signs following" if willing vessels surrender themselves to Him. But we have learned that the Holy Spirit performs His greatest works when the people are free to worship with "all their might." Tremendous healings are taking place during our new worship services. The freedom to pour out one's soul before God in the presence of His anointing is life-changing.

A quiet woman we have known and appreciated for years came to me recently saying, "I have had a bondage for thirty-five years, but now I've been set free!"

What silent misery had she endured? We do not know. This we know—that she is dancing before the Lord, smiling and worshiping with all of her might.

Chaos is never God's way. But what men have come to call "decent church order" and what men call "disorderly emotional issue" (which is believed to result only in chaos) is not biblically accurate! What the Church has called order for the past seventeen hundred years is actually "tradition" that has developed over time through carefully controlled "programs." And who can deny it? Programmed services are orderly. But whose order is it? Is it not the controlled order of the minister under the direction of the "program" which he or his church fathers have constructed?

There is nothing disorderly about a worship service being conducted by a minister under the direction of the Holy Spirit. Disorder occurs when no one is in charge, when no one knows what to do and when everyone is left to himself. What the Apostle Paul sought to correct at Corinth was each person expressing himself without regard to anyone else. In our services Pastor Paul always remains visible. Together, he and I are continually bringing understanding about what is taking place.

The Apostle Paul makes it clear that all spiritual manifestations are subject to the person. No one "has" to do anything at any given moment. The spirits of the prophets are subject to the prophets. Each must, in fact, wait his or her turn so that all may benefit by what God is doing in their midst! God is not the author of confusion, but of peace (see 1 Cor. 14:32-33).

Maintaining Order During Manifestations

What happens then when joy erupts in a church meeting? Or when many fall to the floor under the power of the Spirit? To believers who have never seen the Holy Spirit tangibly manifesting himself, such demonstrations may look chaotic. If, however, there is a minister to whom the people can look for explanation and direction—a minister who is surrendered to and following the leadership of the Holy Spirit—divine order will be maintained. Would we dare suggest that the Holy Spirit is less trustworthy as an orderly leader than a pastor or a printed program?

Despite coming from a traditional background, Paul and I have conducted our worship services under the leadership of the Holy Spirit for sixteen years. During this time we have had to address some disorderly behavior and off-base words of "prophecy." But this has not caused us to quench the true stream of the Holy Spirit from flowing in our midst. Without our realizing it, however, we too had fallen victim to a rigid program. I literally sat with one eye on the clock and felt pressured to release the people "on time." Whose time, indeed?

Now that the Spirit has come with a fresh outpouring, we are finding ourselves flowing quite smoothly with a refreshing change of format. We've broken out of a stagnant mold we had unwittingly fallen into, and almost overnight, our church has come vibrantly alive. We have extended our services by at least an hour, to everyone's delight, and we have become an excited team of witnesses. For ten years we had been encouraging our people to go into the marketplace and witness, but few paid any attention. Now they are going out with no prompting. Salvation and rededication are occurring regularly during our services.

A young businessman came smiling down the corridors one morning, "I just led this man to Christ. He'll be bringing his girl friend on Sunday!" Another came in saying, "My aunt led five people to the Lord on Saturday." In restaurants, in parking lots, around television sets with a "revival" video, people are talking about what is happening. We never hold a meeting now that does not have someone present who has not been in church for years!

That spiritual hunger to see God changing lives, that hope that every true minister longs to see fulfilled, has finally become a reality in the pews. When we come together to worship now, we have something to be excited about—we are winning battles against the opposition of the world! And we are enjoying a taste of victory that we have no hesitation making known to all.

The Natural Posture of Victory

Some people feel that hands raised upward with shouts of victory is disorderly. But every two to four years we watch the Olympics and as each athlete successfully completes his or her medal performance, what posture does he or she take? Hands go high in the air, along with the hands of every member of the family and friends. Why do we throw up our hands and applaud? It is posture of victory! It is natural for people to use their hands and voices at the sight of triumph. To express nothing would not only be discouraging to the victor, it would be unnatural.

What about Jesus' triumph and victory—our wonderful Savior who gave His life to win over Satan? What does He enjoy seeing when His people come together? Shouts! Praises! Arms lifted high and hands applauding the great things He has done, is doing and will continue doing for them!

67

Inviting a Supernatural Invasion

God is spirit, and as the Creator of all nature, He is greater than His creation. You could say He is "Super Nature." Therefore, when natural men on earth pray and invoke the help of God for revival, they are in essence asking for a supernatural invasion of the Holy Spirit.

Knowing this, then isn't resistance to His supernatural movings not only inappropriate, but ridiculous? Why should I reject that which I, by worship and prayer, have invited to come? Who am I to judge whether or not God is behaving decently and in order?

Any time the Spirit manifests himself, He is God and He is going to act like God. I believe the Church has forgotten what God is really like—what unusual things He is likely to perform here on earth. What is it that God has not demonstrated about His willingness to intervene in the affairs of man? Are we talking about the God of Moses and Joshua when we say God does not manifest himself in unusual ways on the earth? The God of Elijah? The God of Elisha? The God of Paul? The God of Peter?

People are forever debating the possibility of spiritual manifestations in today's Church. A young man came up to me after a service recently to say, "My professors say that God only performs supernaturally in order to get a thing established. For example, He brought Israel into Canaan with great signs, and then He ceased doing them. He let the Israelites go on their own to establish themselves, and He did nothing supernatural for four hundred years from Malachi to Matthew. He did the same when He established the Church. First there was Pentecost, then the Church was established and now we don't need miracles and manifestations of the Holy Spirit. We're established." He smiled triumphantly as he then asked me, "What do you think?"

"Baloney!"

"How can you say that?" he said in disbelief.

"Baloney!" I repeated. "I know my Bible too well to

agree with any such theory as that. I have taught Old Testament Survey at Kaleo Bible Institute for years, and I can't think of a book in the Bible where God didn't show His mighty power to His people. Besides that, the Church has to be established fresh in every generation. People are born unsaved and therefore are in need of spiritual convincing every generation. What kind of God would do great things for one generation to show that He can, but refuse to do it for another generation with the same needs?"

Old Questions

- Can God?
- Has God?
- Will God?

These very questions are the bones of contention that keep resurfacing in every fresh outpouring of the Holy Spirit. What keeps these tired questions circulating from generation to generation, outpouring to outpouring? They come out of man's overestimation of his role in the movings of God.

Creation is the design of God. Man did not initiate the world and then invite God to police the problem areas. All the works of men, from beginning to end, were carefully and brilliantly detailed by the Godhead. Not one of us has been chosen by God because of our ability to run things. But we were designed by Him and placed on earth to participate in helping to carry out His agenda. God designed and gave life to each person to fulfill His own plans.

> For we are His workmanship, created in Christ Jesus for good works, which God prepared beforehand that we should walk in them (Eph. 2:10 NKJV).

We are created for His good works that God specifically planned for us to do before we ever existed. We might compare this incredible plan to that of an entrepreneur who conceived a great idea and then went out and raised up and trained men to carry out his vision.

In reality, these "good works" are "God works" initiated and performed by the Holy Spirit. A believer witnesses, a preacher preaches, a saint prays—but nothing happens unless the Holy Spirit moves supernaturally upon the lives of those who hear. If God does it, He owes man nothing. If man does it without God, it is worth nothing.

God is a God of order, but He is not a God of man-initiated programs and methods that control His Spirit. Man-birthed order and programs will not produce spiritual moves or spiritual results. Obedience to the Spirit will produce decency and order along with mighty spiritual moves and powerful spiritual results! It is flesh, not the Holy Spirit, that needs to be regulated.

Ministers and musicians should go into a service skilled, polished and prepared to the best of their ability, but if anything truly spiritual is to be done, the Spirit must be allowed to move in whatever direction He desires. The Church belongs to the supernatural God and no human agent has the right to touch what belongs to Him. God help us to take our hands off the Ark of God!

True decency and order is when God is allowed to be God to His people.

7

Putting Your Hand to the Plow

We are the vessels through which God has chosen to manifest himself, but the program is God's alone. It is God who decides in each generation what nations He will touch, what people He will use and how He will use them. Abraham, Moses, the Apostle Paul, Martin Luther, John Wesley—these men and countless others were raised up to spearhead moves of God in their generations. But the program and the baton has always been God's.

Who's In Charge?

Understanding who is in charge is crucial to flowing with fresh streams of revival when they come. It is God who designs the work and personality of each revival—its theme and the signs of confirmation that will accompany it. A genuine revival will disrupt a church's status quo and God, not man, will decide how the disruptions will proceed. Revivals target churches intentionally, literally invading them.

Some may consider this statement almost heretical, but as great as past revivals were, we will never deepen our relationship with our heavenly Father by studying historical accounts of them. We need to personally experience the manifestations of the Holy Spirit as surely as ancient Corinth or Colosse did. What sins or sicknesses did they have that we do not have more abundantly? I believe Paul would preach the same message to us today that he preached in the first century A.D. I also believe he would perform the same miracles. Could not Paul have been speaking to us today when he warned the Colossian Christians:

> Beware lest any man spoil [rob] you through philosophy [human reasonings against the gospel] and vain deceit, after the tradition of men, after the rudiments of the world [principles and ways contrary to God], and not after Christ (Col. 2:8 KJV).

This is a warning that applies as much to religious traditions and philosophies that try to hinder or limit the power of God's Spirit as it applies to the atheist who disagrees with the existence of God. Jesus warned that anything spoken against Him personally could be forgiven, but anything spoken against the Holy Spirit would never be forgiven, even in eternity. It is serious business to try to hinder what God, by the supernatural work of His Spirit, has determined to do. It can cost a person his life and in some cases even his soul.

God always triumphs. God's people who follow Him should always triumph as well:

> Now thanks be unto God, which always causeth us to triumph in Christ, and maketh manifest the savour [odor] of his knowledge by us in every place (2 Cor. 2:14 KJV).

The phrase *causes us to triumph* becomes even more emphatic when you understand the original words Paul used. Causes (Greek: *triamvus*) means to make a procession of acclamation, to conquer. Triumph (Greek: *aptomai*) means to attach, kindle, set on fire. With this understanding, look again at what Paul is saying about the power in the Church. To paraphrase 2 Corinthians 2:14: "Thanks be unto God who always makes a big parade of us—His conquerors attached to Christ—we are set on fire and made visible, spreading knowledge of Him in every place."

God makes himself known, demonstrates His power visibly through believers, by the person of the Holy Spirit. Why? So that we may show forth and spread the knowledge of Him in every place!

Spiritual Truths—Natural Parallels

Why then should the Church be surprised when supernatural things happen? It should not, of course. The Church should be encouraging itself and whoever it may to joyfully embrace the fresh outpouring of God's grace now cascading over His people. Since sin has clearly gotten its "second wind" in this generation and nothing is held sacred, it was inevitable that the Church would also get a notable infilling of power.

What happens when a plane takes off—or a car starts uphill—or an athlete begins the game? Impetus, additional energy, must be released. Spiritual truths have natural parallels. The Church today needs a fresh impetus. How can we repeat the same ritual for hundreds of years and tell ourselves we are being led by God? Where is the fresh impetus in the Church—that sudden burst of energy that will give us the lead over the world?

Paul and I recently passed a church with a marker on the lawn that read: Service 11:00 A.M.—Sermon 11:30 A.M. "What if the Holy Spirit should have something else in mind for this church?" we wondered aloud.

What if the Holy Spirit should suddenly manifest himself in a new or fresh way in your church? What if He should suddenly manifest himself in a new way in your personal life? Are you really prepared to flow with Him if He chooses to change the direction of your life within the next hour? It is not unlike God to move suddenly in a life:

- God spoke suddenly to Moses (Num. 12:4).
- God uproots the wicked suddenly (Job 5:3).
- At the birth of Jesus, the angel of the Lord was joined suddenly by the host of heaven praising God (Luke 2:13).
- At Pentecost the Holy Spirit came suddenly (Acts 2:2).
- Saul of Tarsus, on his way to persecute believers, was stricken to the ground when a light appeared around him suddenly and the Lord spoke to him (Acts 9:3).

Hands to the Plow

How can men anticipate, program and constrain within time limits such a God who is likely to act suddenly? Jesus once said:

> ...No man, having put his hand to the plough, and looking back, is fit for the kingdom of God" (Luke 9:62 KJV).

What does this have to do with flexibility in adjusting your life or a worship service? When you read the context in which Jesus made this declaration, you will find that He was not talking to unbelievers or backsliders. When Jesus warned about "looking back," He was talking to people who were hesitating about responding to God's present word to them. These believers were not thinking of going back into sin, they were simply hesitant about moving forward with the will of God at that moment.

This is a sobering indictment against anyone in the Church who fails to lean into the forward momentum of the plow to which they have set their hands. Or, to use another Scripture, those who fail to *move with the cloud* of what God is doing at any given time. "Looking back" means to have the knowledge and the power for what the Spirit wants to do, but because of fear of circumstances or man, to look back or turn back, to back away.

Denominational objection, traditional objection, intellectual objection, too much pride—anyone of these excuses for not flowing with the supernatural move of God is the same thing as looking back. When one of the "called" hesitated with the excuse, "Let me first go and bury my father," Jesus responded, *Let the dead bury the dead.*

There are no acceptable excuses to turn back, even temporarily! When God speaks, He knows the full extent of the circumstances around you. It is interesting to note that God never "discusses" His plans with man, He only speaks them. God is not looking to you and me for additional information and He does not need our input to make the best decision. To make anything happen, God only needs our obedience.

When God pours out a river of joy and laughter upon His people, He expects only that we should jump in and became saturated. There is purpose in what He is doing today that extends far beyond the immediate benefit. The Holy Spirit is empowering people, anointing them, for God's work. I like Bill Ligon's definition of the anointing: "Tangible evidence of the manifested presence of God."

Skeptics, hesitaters and procrastinators do not get anointed. Observers who stand on the sidelines with labels and maps, identifying for others what God is doing, do not get anointed. People who are "looking back" get overlooked in any great move of God.

As for myself, I am not only writing about fresh anointing, I am also pressing in for my portion and assignment. As I do, I am praying that I will have the flexibility of a tall stalk of ripe wheat as the breath of God's anointing blows into my life. Anyone who wants to be at the forefront of what God is doing today will have to be willing to make attitude adjustments as the Holy Spirit directs.

The first few days of the "joy meetings," when I was still wondering, the Holy Spirit spoke a very clear word to me: *If you want to be in on this present move of God, you must be willing to adjust on the spot.* He went on to say to my

75

overly-organized, time-conscious mind set, *When you go back to Boston, take everything you had planned to teach in the pulpit for the next few months, set it aside and flow with what I am doing right now.*

Once I determined to do just that, understanding of what God is doing today began to flow. Immediately, I felt an urgency to write this book for the Church so that they too would not hesitate to enter into the moves of the Spirit, for it is He who is moving God's program along to its final resolution of all things foretold in Scripture. I have literally become consumed in revival. God's moves deserve our full cooperation.

Reason For Revival

Aimee Semple McPherson once had a vision which gives one of the best reasons for revivals I have ever read. During the 1930s, the famous evangelist was on her way to China. She had stopped in London, where she was awaiting her ship, when a wealthy man came one evening and insisted she come and speak to a waiting congregation. Surprised to find a vast auditorium of people, Aimee McPherson began to pray when suddenly she found herself caught up "in the Spirit." Under a powerful anointing she saw a healthy, leafy tree with the gifts and fruit of the Holy Spirit on it. As she watched, the tree was totally stripped bare until it became a decayed stump. She then went to Joel 1:4 and read:

> That which the palmerworm hath left hath the locust eaten; and that which the locust hath left hath the cankerworm eaten; and that which the cankerworm hath left hath the caterpillar eaten (KJV).

The Holy Spirit then began to reveal the tree as a picture of the history of the Church. The *palmerworm* came into the freshly empowered Church and ate the *gifts and fruit* (the manifestations) of the Spirit. Without the manifestations of

76

the Spirit, the *locusts* destroyed the *baptism of the Holy Spirit.* Without the anointing of the Holy Spirit, the *cankerworm* attacked the *holy life.* The *caterpillar* attacked the heart of the Gospel—*the new birth.* The perfect tree which had once stood clothed with the power and glory of the Holy Spirit now had little more than a well-developed form of religion.

Standing before her London audience, Mrs. McPherson then saw in her vision the restoration of the Church as God began to take it from the Dark Ages of spiritual barrenness into the age of the Reformations. God raised up John Huss, Martin Luther, John Wesley and others like Kathryn and William Booth and Charles Finney—and the holiness that the cankerworm had taken away began to be restored.

Following the rebirth of the message of holiness came the Welsh Revival and a series of great evangelists, D.L. Moody, Billy Sunday, and Billy Graham. Preaching under the power of the Holy Spirit, millions were converted and the message of the new birth was restored to the Church. Again God poured out His Spirit—this time in Pentecostal power. The doctrine of the baptism of the Holy Spirit was restored to the Church. Joel's prophecy had come full circle:

> And I will restore to you the years that the locust hath eaten, the cankerworm, and the caterpillar, and the palmerworm, my great army which I sent among you. (Joel 2:25 KJV).

(Information partially taken from *Lost and Restored* by Aimee Semple McPherson).

Restoration of Power

A guarantee of full restoration of the Spirit to the Church was finally set in motion. The full Gospel, the full power, was being restored to the Church of the last days of human history! Within this century, both the Church and the nation of Israel began to take on new foliage and fruit. The Church was reinstated with supernatural vision for a great end time harvest of souls for the Kingdom of heaven. Israel was reinstated as host for the coming King and the Kingdom age of the Messiah for one thousand years. The Millennium is near.

This is the day of the "last rains" before the final harvest. This is the time when the Spirit is being poured out with multiple anointings. Signs and wonders are occurring as witnesses to the certainty of our Lord's soon return. Politically speaking, Israel has her hand to the plow. She has set the stage for the last great attack of the Gentiles upon her. The times of the Gentiles will die at Armageddon.

The Spirit is being poured out upon the Church in order to release the anointing that is resident within each believer. The Apostle John said that *the anointing which ye have received of him abideth in you....* This is that river of living water which Jesus said would spring out of those who believe.

Why are signs and wonders necessary today in a Church that is already filled with believers? They alert us to the fact of the presence of God. They are the Church's "knock at the door." When signs begin to appear, the pulpit and pew both have a responsibility to get up from their routine and welcome their visitation until everything has been accomplished that God intended. Remaining open to the signs and wonders is essential to flowing with the evidences of the present moving of the Spirit.

To ignore or disallow the signs and insist on the status quo will hinder and possibly stop the flow altogether in a person's life or in a church. The hard truth of revivals is that they can be quenched, even stopped, by the interference of man. History shows that Jonathan Edward's capitulation to fellow pastors' criticisms stopped the first "awakening" dead in its tracks for four years.

Many churches have a fresh visitation from God only to let it die away after three or four meetings. This should not be. God is visiting the Church in order to stir and awaken us out of our slumber, to stir up the resident anointing within each believer. This means the fresh anointing of the revival—the Reviver—must be taught, preached, talked and proclaimed until His visitation is thoroughly understood and accommodated in our worship services. A Church that does not deal with the fact of the supernatural and make room for its various manifestation in the days ahead is going to become painfully ineffective.

Let us put our hands to the plow and enter in for the great revival that must precede the great harvest.

8

Signs of His Coming

In 1985, something occurred on the international scene that caused quite a stir. An author by the name of Salmon Rushdie wrote a novel around Mohammed and the Islamic religion. He named the book *Satanic Verses.* As a result of the book's publication, the nation of Iran issued a death warrant for Rushdie and has forced him to live in hiding ever since, protected by the British government.

During an interview, Rushdie was asked the question, "Do you believe there is a God?" He replied:

> No, I want to keep an open mind. To believe in God limits the intellect. I want to be free to investigate and pursue ideals as far as the creative mind can go.

My question to Mr. Rushdie's response is this: "Does doubt allow for more freedom of thought than faith? Is doubt not a belief system, a framework of thought as surely as faith?"

In reality, doubt gives man no more access to investigate life than does faith. An atheist has no more access to the world than a minister of the Gospel. Each simply takes different approaches to the same set of information. Atheism does not open some magic door that gives one access to new planets, new humanoids, new circumstances which have been held back from those who would believe in God.

We all breathe the same air, look at the same moon, journey along with the same pathway of human tragedies and triumphs. It is a deception to think that religious skepticism somehow opens new vaults of discovery for a select few.

Faith Never Limits

To think that the finite, created imagination of a human being would be limited by faith in the infinite Creator is embarrassingly egotistical. Faith in God would limit me? What world did I create? Where did I get the raw materials to make something from nothing? What animal kingdom did I design? Was I consulted in the spacing of the stars, moons and planets? The psalmist had the right perspective when he said:

> When I consider the heavens, the work of thy fingers,
> the moon and the stars, which thou hast ordained; what is
> man, that thou art mindful of him? (Ps. 8:3,4 KJV).

I believe atheism severely limits man's intellectual explorations. The atheist is cut off from a vast wealth of information available only to those who enter into true wisdom and knowledge through "faith." Even if man could unravel all the mysteries of earth (which he cannot!) and he missed the mystery of God, what would he have gained? Who but a fool would look only at *The Nightwatch* when Rembrandt sat in next room with the door open?

God himself is more than enough to challenge and entertain the human imagination for the next billion years. Intellectual fear of faith in God is really an internal battle for the throne of one's life. Men deny God because they do not want to be dethroned from being "God" unto themselves.

Rushdie, an excellent communicator of what he believes, went on to say:

> What I don't understand is how a nation can set itself up to be judge and executioner of freedom of thought in a modern society. Martin Scorsese produced a movie which offended many Christians, yet he was allowed to do so. Why cannot I also write with equal liberty around an Islamic setting?

The answer to this question is simple if you are a believer and know the Scriptures. Satan is less tolerant than God. God is *long-suffering, not willing that any should perish but that all should come to repentance.* On the other hand, Satan is void of patience and desires that all perish as miserably as possible.

When Salmon Rushdie touched the Islamic stronghold, he touched the nerve of Satan's end-time strategy. Satan's last great effort to rule the world from Jerusalem will find its greatest ally in the Islamic belt that reaches from India to North Africa. Upon the very spot where the Son of God is destined to sit enthroned, there is presently a gold-domed mosque that has written upon it a quote from the *Koran*: "God has no son." Rushdie touched one of the great powers of the forthcoming Antichrist.

Even so, God is also now touching His great end-time army—just one of the many divine touches the Church and Israel will receive in the days ahead. According to the Scriptures, Jesus' return to earth will be preceded by various signs and wonders of a supernatural nature that will challenge the mind of man—even the Church—in preparation for the final struggles between the Kingdom of God and the kingdom of spiritual darkness.

The Church's Resistance

The Church, amazingly so, has somewhat the same problem as Salmon Rushdie. Anything outside the traditionally religious sphere of the Church is politely, and sometime not so politely, rejected. Historically, great awakenings are invariably resisted by the very Church that purports to want revival.

83

Although earnestly praying for another "Charles Finney awakening," the churches in New England have been subdued by two very real principalities for more than one hundred years: Intellectualism (mind worship) and cultural traditions (ancestor worship). Both have dominated this area for decades, leaving the Church little room in which to have a spiritual impact. New England did not gain the title "minister's graveyard" because of its lively spiritual activities!

In the past ten years, there have been a number of sizable prayer rallies where believers have sought God for a spiritual breakthrough in New England. Yet, when the news spread that revival had broken out in our church, some of the more notable prayer warriors looked at us the way the one hundred and twenty were viewed at Pentecost: "They are drunk on new wine."

I must confess that I believe this observation has been made out of exactly the same offended sense of pride that I felt when I first saw what God is doing today in this new revival. The initial reaction to seeing believers getting up and making a "spectacle" of themselves is difficult to accept from a natural perspective. To be honest, Paul and I were "turned-off" by all the uninhibited expressions of joy and worship we saw taking place. But once it began to happen to us and to people we know, it now makes all the sense in the world.

One young man in our congregation fell out under the power of the Spirit during a meeting. When he finally stood to his feet once again, a microphone was put to his mouth for an explanation. "What happened to you?" he was asked. But the young man was unable to speak, though he earnestly tried to for the next five minutes. This 6'4" former basketball player and college graduate stood speechless, dumbfounded by the Spirit of God. Finally he gave a barely coherent explanation of his feelings and sat down.

Previously, this same young man had been making the decisions for his life based on what he wanted. Only in recent months had he gotten down to the serious business of trying to get the mind of God. I believe God was trying to help him by showing him a greater power than mental preparedness and natural desires.

Another couple we know, who have every reason to be totally heartbroken as their only son was recently sentenced to several years in a maximum security prison for drug crimes, has broken out into dancing and uncontrollable laughter on several occasions. During these times of fresh anointing, God has been speaking wonderful things to their understanding, carrying them along their journey.

No one would guess their reasons for pain, but everyone knows their reasons for joy. God is touching their lives in very real ways. In spite of the natural, painful circumstances they are living out, they have a joy that is making sense out of their lives and they are ministering that joy to others. There is not a service that goes by that one or both of them are not actively involved in reaching out to others. The result has been not only strengthening for them but their son has requested a Bible and he has asked them to forgive him.

At one point in a morning service, when everything was quiet and sweet with an atmosphere of gentleness, a substantial woman whom we all love stood up to give a testimony. When she would have begun talking, she began instead to gently laugh. With a line here and there infused with generous joy, she finally looked at us helplessly and then doubled over with laughter saying, "Who cares! I haven't had a drink in years!" With that the entire congregation broke up.

This same woman we now call "a walking doxology" is a person with a very painful past which included much rejection and a drinking habit. But the sweet worship that now comes from this spiritually intoxicated woman is like a balm to the soul. At one moment in a particular service when Pastor Bill Ligon was praying "The Father's Blessing" on every member of the congregation, and people were dropping to the floor all over the sanctuary, I overheard our "walking doxology" behind me saying:

85

I've never seen anything like it in my life. Oh, Father, what a privilege to be able to experience your Presence. What a moment for the children to be a part of. We are all so blessed by You, Father.

And she is right. This is indeed an awesome moment in Divine history. Jesus is coming again. What a shame to let the principalities of "mind worship" and "ancestor worship" rejoice because we would not "enter in" to the Church's preparation for the coming of The King.

Celebrate His Return!

When John the Baptist leaped in his mother's womb at the sight of Jesus in Mary's womb, he experienced a joy that will reach its fulfillment only at the second coming of Jesus. John explains as much when he said:

> He that hath the bride is the bridegroom: but the friend of the bridegroom, which standeth and heareth him, rejoiceth greatly because of the bridegroom's voice; this my joy, therefore, is fulfilled (John 3:29 KJV).

In his gospel writing, John used a custom of the day as an analogy, where the best man stood outside the bridal chamber to hear the first words of the groom's delight in his bride. John was speaking prophetically that his joy would be full on the day when Jesus joins with His bride for eternity. Then John invited all of us to join in the celebration:

> Let us be glad and rejoice and give Him glory, for the marriage of the Lamb is come, and His wife has made herself ready (Rev. 19:7 NKJV).

The expected coming of Messiah was the basis for the joy of ancient Israel:

> Rejoice greatly, O daughter of Zion! Shout, O daughter
> of Jerusalem! Behold, your King is coming to you; He is
> just and having salvation, lowly and riding on a donkey, a
> colt, the foal of a donkey (Zech. 9:9 NKJV).

The Church has lost the joy of the Lord because it has
lost the heart of the Gospel. In a world filled with so much
death and disappointment, we forget we are a people with a
guarantee of life—salvation is our trademark. We of all
people have cause to celebrate. But we have become so
spiritual! We have even made a somber memorial service out
of the Lord's Supper, which was originally a meal of
celebration (see Acts 2:47.). People who want proof of God
should be able to come into a congregation and experience
an attitude of celebratory worship around His Word that
would make a Super Bowl football game seem dull!

Rejoice With God

The destiny of God's people is joy, laughter, and
celebration in all of their divine assignment—God himself
being the Chief Celebrant among us:

> I will rejoice in Jerusalem, and joy in My people; the
> voice of weeping shall no longer be heard in her, nor the
> voice of crying (Isa. 65:19 NKJV).

Imagine God rejoicing! It would be like a thousand
nuclear warheads, all going off at once. John said in the Book
of Revelation that Jesus' voice sounded like the roaring of
many waters. Imagine when God begins to laugh and
celebrate with His people!

When the wise men of the East saw the stellar announcement of the birth of the Great King, *they rejoiced with
exceeding great joy.* Isaiah told God's people to *cry out and
shout, O inhabitant of Zion, for great is the Holy One of
Israel in your midst!* (Isa. 12:6 NKJV).

The problem with the Church today is lifelessness! We may have the correct doctrine. We have built impressive buildings. We have many beautiful and meaningful expressions of worship. But too often we are caught up in a religious routine that matures and empowers no one for worship or works with tangible evidence. Oh, come Holy Spirit, we need you!

We have reached the time in history where sin is being allowed its full expression and we have let the very supernatural life that created the Church ebb out of our midst. Who will take the mantle of anointing and say with Elisha, "Where is the God of Elijah?"

Signs and Wonders Reinforce the Message

To be made alive in spirit by the Holy Spirit of God is fundamental to every other valid, spiritual experience. Spiritual birth gives man access to a relationship with the living God. Second in order of importance to our salvation and restored relationship to God is our relationship o one another as people of God. It is upon and through this essential foundation the Holy Spirit moves and carries out the program of God.

The Church has labored and guided seeking people for the past two thousand years. Salvations, restoration of relationships and charitable deeds have resulted. This is good spiritual fruit. But this is not signs and wonders.

The Church is composed of people through whom God desires to demonstrate His presence with sign and wonders. Even a pagan king observed this twenty-five hundred years ago. With Daniel in his court, Darius of Mede issued a public decree throughout his kingdom that God *worketh signs and wonders in heaven and in earth* (Dan. 6:27 KJV). I find it amazing that a pagan king perceived the works of the Holy Spirit better than so many of the people today, even those who are filled with the Spirit.

Signs and wonders reinforce the message that Jesus in

coming again—this time to rule as King. There will be many events in the days to come that will baffle those who worship human understanding and logic. I would like to share with you now two such baffling events that have occurred recently in our meetings. The first I call, "The Miracle of Robert Cohen."

The Miracle of Robert Cohen

In the middle of a service one evening, one of our deacons came with a letter saying, "This man wants to give a testimony."

I walked to the back of the auditorium where Robert Cohen and his wife were seated (total strangers to me), and brought them forward. "Tell us the story behind this letter," I urged.

A middle-aged, stocky man, looking the picture of health, said,

> I was diagnosed with cancer in both lungs. After much prayer, surgery was performed and then I took several months of chemotherapy. I was pronounced clear of cancer. A short time later the cancer returned, my lymph nodes became swollen, and I was discouraged. Prayer was ministered for me continually, especially by my wife. Then someone told us to come to the Christian Teaching and Worship Center and perhaps God would speak to me about my condition.
>
> I came to the service one evening and Pastor Paul called me out for prayer. As I was standing there, Mona walked over, laid her hand on my chest and said, "God is going to do a great work in this man. Do not have any doubt. Do not have any fear." She then turned to my wife and said, "The Lord has heard your request. What you have been praying for is within your reach. The Lord has spread His skirts of protection over your family and you will be blessed."

The following letter tells the rest of the story:

89

MASSACHUSETTS GENERAL HOSPITAL — HARVARD MEDICAL SCHOOL
THE MGH CANCER CENTER

ROBERT W. CAREY, M.D.
Medical Oncology Unit

The Cox Buildin
Blosson Stree
Boston, Massachuset
Tel. (617) 26-86
Fax (617) 23-77

January 3, 1994

John Wain, M.D.
Warren 11
Massachusetts General Hospital

RE: Robert Cohen
    212-02-62

Dear John,

We certainly have a surprising situation with Mr. Robert Cohen. He had six months of chemotherapy ending in the fall of 1992, and then a recurrence in the right upper lobe prompted additional radiation therapy which has been completed. His chest CT of 9/29/93 showed radiation changes and no discrete parenchymal nodules. He seems to have been rendered completely free of the multiple nodules that he had. He feels well. His weight is up to 204.

On examination the neck is supple. The thyroid is normal. The lungs are clear. The liver and spleen are not enlarged. There is no adenopathy in any location. There are no heart murmurs.

Impression: No evidence of disease at this time.

Plan: Follow-up at three month intervals.

RWC/dl/TR

Robert W. Carey, M.D.

cc: Noah Choi, M.D.
    Cox 302

To God be all the glory! The second event of signs and wonders I want to relate is the story of a tiny, bubbly blond wife and mother named Donna. Probably no cameras will ever come to feature her story, but Donna represents millions of church goers who exemplify true Christianity and what happens to them in times of revival.

A "Sign" Named Donna

When the economic slump hit Massachusetts in 1990, Donna's husband was released from his job in engineering along with thousands of other qualified men and women. Unemployed, with no income and two small children, Donna found it necessary to seek a job. Being unskilled, she found work in private and institutional care of the elderly. She took care of their failing bodies, their failing emotions and their failing environment.

Instead of resenting her sudden misfortune and new responsibilities, Donna saw her job as an opportunity for ministry. Within three years, Donna has led more than ninety elderly men and women into a personal relationship with Jesus Christ, the majority whose precious souls are now in eternity. When Donna walks into a nursing home, its patients glow with happiness, but none glow more so than Donna. She loves her seniors.

When the revival broke out in our church, I wanted to see Tom and Donna enter into the refreshing. They needed and deserved it. But they sat and watched. Then one day I saw them coming down to the altar during the ministry. Later on in the evening I noticed Donna still there, leaning forward laughing. When we left the service that night at 11:15, Donna was still in the exact same position.

I learned the next day that Donna was so saturated in the power of the Spirit, she had to be "assisted" from the sanctuary. As a result, both Tom and Donna are walking in a new liberty. "It's not that our circumstances have changed," said Tom, "but the fact that my work situation is not what it was is no longer the focus of my life. I feel much lighter and more God-centered now."

Donna then made an unusual observation that many of us have experienced, but had not verbalized as such. "Have you noticed a change in your sleep?" she questioned. "When I wake up in the morning it is like I have been ministered to throughout the night. I just close my eyes in revival and the next thing I know, I am awake—in revival! It's hard to explain, but it's changing me."

Sweet, divinely touched sleep—who would have expected it? People who have lost jobs, positions, businesses, relationships—God is restoring and refreshing the tired, discouraged, overworked sheep of His pasture. And many of our people are receiving valid dreams from God during their sleeping hours. Solomon said of the blessed:

> When thou liest down, thou shalt not be afraid: yea, thou shalt lie down, and thy sleep shall be sweet (Prov. 3:24 KJV).

Donna is among them. She is one of the handmaids about whom Joel prophesied more than twenty-six hundred years ago:

> ...And upon the handmaids in those days [the last days] will I pour out my spirit (Joel 2:29 KJV).

As a footnote to her spiritual blessings, Donna was also subsequently hired to an outstanding position at a prestigious hospital! As she gave me the news, I saw that her mission had remained the same—souls for the kingdom.

9

Shout

When I awoke one morning, this word immediately popped into my mind—SHOUT!

That is exactly what the Word of God tells us to do. SHOUT about the goodness and the glory of our God. Nowhere in the Bible are we told to whisper the secrets of our God between ourselves in quiet little groups. No, we're told to SHOUT about the power of the name of God to all.

The world hates the sound of God, and the Church unfortunately continues to be intimidated and therefore victimized by what the world thinks. Yet the world quickly shouts, yells, blows horns, marches in parades, forms fan clubs, rolls out the red carpet, claps, interviews and publicly acknowledges its causes for celebration. The Church on the other hand sits quietly with muffled voices, an occasional cough, and well-rehearsed recitations—all the while proclaiming its reason for celebration. But not too loudly, please!

Emotionalism! Emotionalism!

There certainly are times for quiet reflection and meditation before God in our church services, but worship services are also times of generous celebration. There is a time to be public with what God has done, is doing and will do. These assemblies of the believers are the times for supernatural demonstrations and joyous testimonies of genuine victories over life's circumstances.

The universe was created as a praise unto God. The Church fathers declared that the chief end of man is to glorify God. The natural state of man is to praise. This very state of praise has two sides, however. Because we are designed to praise, if we do not praise God—we praise ourselves.

The world has ridiculed the Church, telling it that it is unsophisticated to be loud or spiritually demonstrative. Religious critics have often hit the Church with cries of, "Emotionalism! Emotionalism!" And the Church has believed them. This may sound like a paradox, but shame on us for having become ashamed to shout over our spiritual victories. While the world makes a boisterous noise unto its "gods of flesh," we often sit quietly by hoping that God enjoys our reverent respect.

God is not afraid of noise. God himself is unabashedly loud at times.

> Then the Lord awakened as one out of sleep, and like a mighty man that shouted by reason of wine. And he smote his enemies in the hinder parts [He kicked His enemies in the pants!]: he put them to a perpetual reproach (Ps. 78:65.66 KJV).

The word shout in the original Hebrew is *ranah*. It means to exult, rejoice greatly, be overjoyed, running over with joy. Something that runs over draws attention. When it's joy that is running over, how can such a spilling forth be done in secret? (A letter came from a radio interview I once did which said, "I appreciate your understanding of eschatology, but you need to rethink your attitude on worship. You almost sound charismatic!" I hope so!

The Vehicle of Emotion

Let us take another look at the three words in the original Greek language that express human joy:

- *Chairo:* Physical comfort and well-being.
- *Euphraino:* Subjective (self-reflective) feeling of joy.
- *Agalliaomai:* Outward demonstration of joy and pride and the exultation experienced in public worship.

Emotion is not an expression; it is a vehicle of expression. As a veteran who climbed out of the pit of fear and depression some years ago, I learned that any number of feelings can be channeled through the vehicle we call emotions. Anger, joy, selfishness, giving—we choose to a great extent what we entertain and allow emotionally. Some things God has left up to us, and our emotional state is one thing that is largely in our hands.

I learned this after two emotional near-collapses. The responsibility to choose sound thoughts by feeding our minds healthy food from God's Word is basically ours. It was a choice I learned that I had to make daily.

Emotion Explained

Emotion is a part of our makeup created by God. It is the vehicle for our words that help to make our inner selves known. In its best and highest state, emotion gives glory to God.

Emotion is a vehicle for joy which is one of the spiritual fruit (see Gal. 5:22,23) that is to be expressed during worship. Spiritual joy is not a display of human feelings, rather it is spiritual expression of divine happiness. When these expressions are brought forth within the Church under the leadership of the Holy Spirit, they are always appropriate, pleasing to God, energizing, healing and restorative.

We need spiritual joy that erupts into shouts from time

to time, and we need to let the world hear it. As the Church, we have this great weapon in our hands. Let us not be so hesitant to employ it. We need to pick up the shout of God and use it! True joy is God's primary method of infusing our lives with fresh energy from heaven.

Let us look for a moment at the use of the word shout in the Scriptures and see what God says about it:

> O clap your hands, all ye people; shout unto God with the voice of triumph (Ps. 47:1 KJV).

When Israel came out of Egypt, they had no king as other nations. Yet, they were organized, armed, able to fight, conquer and be delivered. Why? Because, as Moses said first, and then Joshua repeated, Israel knew about shouting:

> ...The Lord his God is with him [Jacob/Israel], and the shout of a king is among them (Num. 23:21 KJV).

> And it shall come to pass, that when they make a long blast with the ram's horn, and when ye hear the sound of the trumpet, all the people shall shout with a great shout; and the wall of the city [Jericho] shall fall down flat, and the people shall ascend up every man straight before him (Josh. 6:5 KJV).

David believed in shouting:

> ...Let all those that put their trust in thee rejoice: let them ever shout for joy, because thou defendest them... (Ps. 5:11 KJV).

> Be glad in the Lord, and rejoice, ye righteous: and shout for joy, all ye that are upright in heart (Ps. 32:11 KJV).

> Arise, O Lord, into thy rest; thou, and the ark of thy strength. Let thy priests be clothed with righteousness; and let thy saints shout for joy (Ps. 132:8,9 KJV).

96

The prophets Zephaniah and Zechariah believed in shouting:

> Sing, O daughter of Zion; shout, O Israel; be glad and rejoice with all the heart [mind, will, emotion]... (Zeph. 3:14 KJV).

> Rejoice greatly, O daughter of Zion; shout, O daughter of Jerusalem: behold, thy King cometh unto thee... (Zech. 9:9 KJV).

The people of God have cause to shout! We are kept by the Lord of joy. And He is coming again with the shout of a King—a shout that will drown out all opposing voices.

Reason to Hope

Let us throw off the spirit of heaviness so prevalent in our day. There is reason to hope, to rejoice, to release the wells of joy within our souls to become a well-watered garden. No longer are we a sin-parched wasteland. No longer are we a backslidden people cut off from God. No longer do we have to be overcome by addictions, or failures, like an army with no weapons. Everyone of us has a mighty weapon within us—we have a shout within our souls that nothing can stand before.

One young woman in our congregation was going through a painful family situation to the extent she developed an ulcer, lost excessive weight, sank into a depression that added ten years to her face and caused her to become virtually non-functional. During a service one evening, we began to rejoice in songs and shouts of praises until the entire sanctuary rang. Someone grabbed the hand of the depressed young woman and began to leap down the aisles with her. By the time they arrived back at their seat the heaviest oppression over her had been broken. She has had to continue to walk out her painful situation, but she will make it! That overwhelming feeling of despair that had almost smothered her is now gone. The shout of the Holy Spirit pierced the enemy's blanket of despair.

We arrived at the church one evening and heard the sound of a loud voice pouring out of the office windows. To our amazement, it was our daughter Susan. Since the revival had come to our church Susan had been pressing in, flowing in faith but not experience. She was hungry to be visited by the mighty Spirit of God. Finally He came and for the next full week, we in the offices thought we would be forced to buy ear plugs. Her naturally piercing shouts went up and down the hallways of the church until no skeptics were left.

We all knew Susan had received a generous drink and her cup was overflowing. As a result of Susan's shouts, countless others who had been observing from a distance began to come to her for the "laying on of hands" with the same infilling of joy. Her joy was infectious, contagious, compelling, visible and life changing!

The most popular phrase to come from her overflowing cup is, "I'll never be the same again." She won't and neither will those she is touching. Susan is rapidly blossoming in the pulpit as a powerful minister, her natural frame now casting an even larger spiritual image. Her shouts are forceful and life piercing. She is moving joyfully and powerfully in this fresh anointing and she is bringing many along with her.

A Man Full of the Holy Ghost

Dr. Hudson Taylor (1832-1905) was a missionary to China. It is said of him that he was:

> ...A man full of the Holy Ghost; entirely surrendered to God; a man of great self-denial, heartfelt compassion, great power in prayer, marvelous organizing ability, energetic, indefatigable, wielding much influence with people...with childlike humility....For forty years the sun never rose on China but Hudson Taylor was on his knees for the salvation of the Chinese.

On one of his furloughs to England in 1855, Hudson Taylor was preaching when he suddenly stopped. He stood speechless for a time with his eyes closed. When he began to speak again he explained:

> I have seen a vision. I saw in this vision a great war that will encompass the whole world. I saw this war recess and then start again, actually being two wars. After this, I saw much unrest and revolts that will affect many nations. I saw in some places spiritual awakenings.
>
> In Russia, I saw there will come a general all-encompassing spiritual awakening so great that there could never be another like it. From Russia I saw the AWAKENING spread to many European countries. Then I saw an ALL OUT awakening followed by the coming of Christ.

> (From an original Russian article titled "Spiritual Revival" published in Finland in 1945. *Hudson Taylor's Spiritual Secret;* Moody Press.)

Spiritual awakenings are slated for the days ahead! This is something to shout about.

Spiritually Visible

The world has became outlandish and ridiculous in its expressions. As one Hollywood motion picture producer said, "The lunatic fringe has now become mainstream." While the Church is not called to become ridiculous, it is called to out-shout its competitors. It is called to be spiritually visible and audible in a fleshy and noisy world.

When our son Joshua-Paul was a senior in one of the more prestigious high schools of the Boston area, of his own accord he took it upon himself to rebut the school's obvious policy of "promoting better understanding of the homosexual lifestyle." Joshua wrote an article on morality entitled "In Defense of Homophobia" that ended up in the town newspaper. The attacks, ridicule and accusations from his peers were plentiful. But in the midst of it all, I observed a wonderful thing take place in Joshua. Instead of becoming intimidated, the attacks actually released a determination within him to press forward with more zeal. It reminded me of the Book of Revelation promise that believers *overcame by the word of their testimony and they loved not their life unto the death.*

The victorious shout is a weapon that works best in the hands of those who are willing to die to self. To those who will risk their reputation, their popularity, their profession, their ministry—their all—for the sake of the will of God, the shout is an arrow shot forth with skill. The world knows when it hears *the shout of a king.* Royalty has a unique sound that is absent in all other parades. Let the King's children rise up with boldness and be heard, royally!

In one of our services, a Greek Orthodox cantor began to sing out during worship. He sang first in Greek, and then he spoke in English. Three times he did this and as his worship went out, our youth minister saw smoke rings going from small to large over the congregation.

The power of the Holy Spirit fell in that moment and wonderful ministry, worship and praise erupted all over the auditorium. People became drunk in the Spirit with laughter, tears or whatever sacrifice they desired to release unto God. It was one of the great shouts to come out of this revival. Truly, people of every tongue and language are entering in and touching the heart of God.

10

Key to Revival

In 1990, I had a dream in which I met three ominous visitors: a woman minister and two men, one being her husband. As soon as I awoke, I knew God was speaking. What He gave to me was a vital key to revival.

In the dream, my husband and I were driving down a familiar road in the country when I remarked, "Do you see that house at the foot of the mountain? The woman minister I was telling you about lives there." No sooner had I said it than we were pulling onto her back lawn. All the vegetation around the house made it appear dimly lit within and claustrophobic. The woman minister emerged and was quite hospitable, but I was anxious to leave.

A few days later, as my husband and I were approaching our house back in Boston, we found a car parked in our driveway. Opening the car door, I looked inside to see the woman minister hanging onto the steering wheel with her eyes almost closed. Suffering from exhaustion, she could hardly introduce the two men traveling with her.

Seeing the woman's obvious condition, I felt compelled to invite her to come into our house and rest. Out of courtesy, I motioned her ahead of me and walked behind her, accompanying her husband. As the woman's husband and I began to casually converse on our way to the house, I suddenly became aware of the outstanding features of this man. As the Bible said of Daniel, he had an excellent spirit which drew people to him.

I wanted to know him better, but all of a sudden he began to quicken his pace and leave me behind. "Wait, I can't go that fast!" I called out. But the excellent man soon disappeared out of sight.

Going into the house, I hoped to find him. But instead, I went directly to the bedroom where the woman was lying down. As we began to talk, I suddenly noticed for the first time just how beautiful she was, especially since she had rested. And I soon forgot all about her husband.

"You're beautiful!" I said to her. "I never realized just how beautiful you are."

Then like a flash she was gone, and the "second man" traveling with the woman was there lying on the bed. He reached up, put his arm around my neck in a demanding way, and bent my head down close to his face. His expression was amiable, but his grip was threatening. And although I felt uncomfortable, I also liked being there. He had a magnetism about him. But even in his grip, my thoughts returned to the excellent husband of the woman. Somehow I knew that, of the three, he was the most rewarding to be with.

As I thought on this, the man who had me by the neck breathed these words into my face, "The woman's husband is responsible for sound doctrine; I am responsible for the business and practical ministrations of the work."

I somehow knew he was referring to the Church and then I woke up. The dream had ended. But I knew that God was trying to tell me something important for His people. Immediately I began to pray for an understanding of my three mysterious visitors. Throughout the day I prayed until late in the afternoon. Then, step by step, God began to pull back the curtain of my understanding with a vital message for those who have been called and ordained to the pulpit.

I believe the message of this dream exposes the primary

cause of ministry burnout, integrity deficit, overextended financial burdens, doctrinal fads and lack of anointed ministry. I believe it is a vital key to the revival and spiritual refreshing from God's presence that is presently being poured out upon the Church.

I submit the dream to all who stand in the esteemed office of those who are called and ordained to be official spokesmen for God. I further submit this message to the entire body of Christ. In principle, it applies to every believer who sincerely desires a more fruitful walk with the Lord Jesus.

The Dream

Going over each scene several times, I tried to remember every detail that might lend significance:

- I was on a familiar, well-traveled main road.

- A woman minister lived in a house at the foot of a mountain.

- The house was overgrown with vegetation and had a closed-in, claustrophobic atmosphere.

- That same woman minister showed up at my house one day with her husband and another man.

- The woman was exhausted.

- Her husband, who was of an excellent spirit, disappeared; and although I sensed that of the three he was the most important, I could never find time to locate him.

- I discovered the woman minister was surprisingly beautiful, but she too disappeared when the "second man" came on the scene.

103

- The "second man" traveling with the woman and her husband grasped me by the neck and would not let go—a position I both liked and disliked.

- This same man said that the husband of the woman was responsible for sound doctrine, but he himself was responsible for the practical ministrations of the work.

Interpretation: The woman represents the ministers of the Gospel. Her husband represents the ministers' call to fellowship with God through prayer, study and ministry of the Word. The second man represents the practical ministrations built around the ministry.

Most of God's ministers live at the foot of the mountain. They are weary, overworked and dry. Planning, policy and business are like vines wrapped around the neck of their ministries which bind them to the practical responsibilities of their call. The call of the minister is to separate himself unto God in order that he may bring God's anointed Word down from the mountain to the people.

Prayer, study and fellowship with God around His Word is the excellent husband of the woman in the dream. He is greater than the minister and more important than the practical responsibilities. Yet, he never lingers or begs to be acknowledged. Fellowship with God waits on the mountain top for anyone who will make the climb, but He will not come down and compete for attention.

The pulpit which God has provided for each minister has one purpose, and that is to make the Word of the King known. It is the only pulpit a minister is ever called to fill and his primary preparation for that pulpit is to dedicate himself to keep his divine appointment on the mountaintop, in the Presence of the Holy One.

Weariness and powerlessness are the result of living at the foot of the mountain. The Word of the Lord never ascends up from the people. It is brought down by those who have been in God's presence, and on whom the fragrance of His glory still lingers.

Human Planning or God's Power?

God's shepherds confer with one another at great expense—traveling, seeking, advising, planning. But real growth and real revival will not come unless there is first intimacy with God. Unless a fear, a reverence, a repentance for absence away from His Presence is corrected, man's plans will continue to be exchanged, but the power will continue to elude the plans!

Unless the Word of God is delivered in the house of God by men and women empowered by being in the Presence of God, the business of man will continue to choke the work of God.

If truth be fallen in the streets, it is only because a lie has been sold to those in the pulpit. This lie tells them that their time will serve them better in the streets, confronting the issues, marketing their wares, outlining their strategies and establishing their goals. And all of this is generally accomplished outside of prayer and communion with the Holy Spirit. Therefore, what often starts out in the Presence of God is finished by the ingenuity of flesh and reaps the results of a small harvest.

The cry of the marketplace rings in the ear of the minister. It says, "Come down from the mountaintop and help us!" But wise men and women of God remain faithful to their call, waiting for the Word to be emblazoned on the tablets of their own hearts. Then he or she descends long enough to pass those tablets on to the priesthood (the laity) who in turn will go into the marketplace of life with words so fresh from the mouth of God that the anointing of His breath is still upon them.

The feeding of the sheep accomplished, the *perfecting of the saints for the work of the ministry* attended to, the minister turns once again and begins the climb back up the mountain in search of a fresh anointing of power for the people. What? No important causes? No special projects to spearhead donation campaigns? Where does he think he is going?

It is important to remember that Jesus neither challenged Rome nor built any hospitals or orphanages. He was very focused on what was and what was not His call. Jesus Christ came to preach the Kingdom. But *those who received His Word* did go into the world arena and overturn great empires and bind up the wounds of the hurting and the poor, building whatever needed to be built!

Every believer is called to an anointed ministry of witness and exhortation in the marketplace. The pulpit is clearly a call to a life of dedication to prayer, study and anointed ministry of the Word that will perfect and build up God's foot soldiers to go out and *tread on the head of the enemy.* God has always had spokesmen to His people who have carried forth a fresh word in every generation. He has them today, as well.

This I believe: When God moves sovereignly to revive His people, those ministers in the pulpit who refuse to flow with His Spirit will be set aside in favor of those who will flow with Him. Laity will be ordained by God to replace the ministers who choose to bow their necks and stiffen their stand against His sovereign movements.

What Is Missing?

• Understanding the purpose of the pulpit.
• Purifying of the pulpit.
• Anointing in the pulpit.

When these three issues are clarified and understood by those who stand in the pulpit, there will be an empowering of God's Spirit flowing out to all believers that will prepare them to be living pulpits in the marketplace of life. This is the number one need facing the Church today: *Anointed*

ministers in the pulpit with the determination to pass on the
anointing to the laity for the work of the ministry.

This is the necessary key to a truly great revival in these
last days. What the world needs most is to see is a Church
aflame with the power of God, and it will when every pulpit
is ablaze with an anointed minister of the Word who
recognizes the true purpose of the pulpit.

Two great moves of God have been sovereignly initiated
by the Holy Spirit in this century. A third is now underway.
Let us not hesitate to make our pulpits available to the Holy
Spirit, bringing the Word from fresh communion with His
fresh anointing. Only then will the world see the God-sized
harvest we have all been expecting.

11

Revival Fires That Keep Burning (Entering In)

How long a "special" outpouring of the Holy Spirit will last, no one ever knows. The amount of individual surrendering and embracing of the Holy Spirit's demonstrations and manifestations is certain to affect the duration of such a move of God. But even if the length of time is shorter than hoped for and many pull back, an anointing of the Holy Spirit moving within a worship service is going to benefit whomever will allow it to touch them.

During these wonderfully refreshing times, people who have never laid hands on anyone find supernatural power being transmitted through them as they pray. People who appear to be only nominal believers may be healed or set free emotionally. The precedent was set thousand of years ago when God took of the anointing that was upon Moses and imparted it to the seventy elders who would assist Moses in the work. As soon as the anointing was imparted, the seventy elders of Israel began to prophesy (see Num. 11:16,25).

Commitment to Continue

If special moves of the Holy Spirit, anointing, healings and blessings from God, have any ongoing benefit in a life, there must be a corresponding commitment of that person to walk in that anointing, that blessing. This occurs by a daily surrender to the Holy Spirit.

Twenty-one years ago, my heart went into fibrillation momentarily. From that day forward my physical and emotional health declined until I reached a point of desperation. After two years of debilitating illness I was wonderfully visited by the Holy Spirit in a definite way. I even knew the exact moment He arrived. An almost indescribable, comforting warmth entered the top of my body and radiated throughout my entire being. It was a tangible visitation I experienced on numerous occasions for the next four months. My health was wonderfully restored.

At seven years of age, my grandson was operated on for the fastest-growing cancer known, Burkitts Lymphoma. It is a rare form of cancer that doubles in size every day. The Holy Spirit imparted the gift of faith (1 Cor. 12:9) to our daughter, and she set her face like a flint—never shedding a tear—to intercede for his life. Today Jeremy is thirteen years old and in perfect health.

Did we receive these two miraculous interventions and others from God, breathe a sigh of gratefulness and relief, and then simply return to our old way of living? No, a thousand times no! The lives of every member of our family were radically changed by these visitations. Our lifestyle was permanently altered and we are not the same people we were before the touch of God.

My husband, who was a university professor, is now a pastor. Our son, who was literally a "beach bum," is now a Bible teacher who has established a Bible school in Latvia. Our son-in-law, who was a nominal Catholic, is an administrator and a pillar in our church. Our little ones have their whole lives built around the Lord.

I share this to represent what I believe God expects to occur in any family or individual life that He has touched. I believe this kind of life-changing response or commitment is precisely what God is looking for in any outpouring of His

Spirit. Whenever God sends spiritual refreshings among His people, He is looking for renewed zeal and commitment. He wants people whose fire has died down and smoldered to suddenly burst up into flame—He wants people to feel the heat of His love and power as they once did at the beginning of their love walk with Him. He wants people who have been beaten down or contaminated by the world to stand up and SHOUT out His name.

God sends His Spirit forth so that His cause may be advanced toward the day of His coming. But God is never so concerned with His cause that He overlooks the building of the character of His people. Because He wants to bless His own, Jesus made it a point to lay down a pattern that applies to every person who will go on to spiritual maturity and fruitfulness. In any move of the Spirit, God is looking for "fruit that remains." God is looking for commitment to continue in what He has given.

The pattern for a spiritually fruitful life was laid down by Jesus in a message we have come to call the Sermon on the Mount. The Sermon on the Mount actually describes the constitution for the Millennium. Its principles not only apply now, but will be the standard of conduct when Jesus reigns from Jerusalem. The beatitudes which open that sermon are the framework for a truly Spirit-led life.

The Beatitudes

Matthew writes of Jesus that:

> ...Seeing the multitudes, he went up into a mountain: and when he was set, his disciples came unto him: and he opened his mouth and taught them, saying, Blessed are the poor in spirit: for theirs is the kingdom of heaven (Matt. 5:1-3 KJV).

In this statement and those following, Jesus makes clear what sustains revival fires within a life and causes men and women to produce fruit that will survive into the age to come.

Matthew begins verse two with the Hebrew phrase, *And he opened his mouth.* This means by translation that Jesus did not draw the multitudes aside to give them a pep talk on the spur of the moment. Rather, He had a "set of the will" as He *opened his mouth* because these were not casual followers. From the tone of the words used in His teaching, Jesus was speaking to people who were serious about learning. They were disciples who were serious enough to handle the bigger picture. Any time the Holy Spirit moves in great power, God is aiming that power at those who will walk with Him in the bigger picture—people who are willing to break out of their present mold and flow with fresh advances of the Holy Spirit.

The word beatitude means blessed. In the original Greek, the word is *makarios* and means supremely blessed, fortunate, well off. In the beatitudes recorded in the Gospel of Matthew, Jesus was not just patting the heads of the poor, saying, "Don't worry, some day, you will be rich." The Sermon on the Mount was never meant to imply that God loves poor people and hates the wealthy. Material goods are not even in question here.

With the multitudes looking on, those disciples who were hungry for "spiritual moves and maturity" drew close to Jesus and pressed in for more. Then Jesus deliberately began to instruct them on the real cost of following Him. His opening statement is the sum total of His entire message. Everything else He says is based on this first line. We who want to be blessed today must recognize the importance of being "poor in spirit" if anything else Jesus said has a chance of happening in our lives.

Blessed Are the Poor in Spirit

Blessed are the poor in spirit... The word poor used here, from the Greek word *ptochos,* means the lowest form of poverty. This poor does not refer to those who must work hard for their daily bread, but rather those who must beg. It does not mean those who have little, but those who have nothing. Combine this poor with spirit, *the poor in spirit,* and it means that citizens of the Kingdom of heaven who are blessed are those who take stock of their inward self and see absolutely nothing of value. It does not mean they are poor in spirit in God's sight, it means that in their own sight they clearly see they are devoid of anything good.

The Apostle Paul said, *I know that in me dwelleth no good thing.* Paul understood the Sermon on the Mount and the vision of the first beatitude. In the face of his brilliant mind and outstanding education, Paul took inventory of himself and found nothing of lasting value. In direct opposition to the modern psychology of today which says, "You are great, good, brilliant and deserving," Paul said to put absolutely no confidence in our own flesh.

> For we are the circumcision, who worship God in the Spirit, rejoice in Christ Jesus, and have no confidence in the flesh (Phil. 3:3 NKJV).

Every pocket of self-confidence in our flesh and ability is like a boulder of opposition set up against God-confidence. If I lean on my flesh, I pull away from God. If I lean toward heaven, I pull away from the world and its standards of self-exaltation. Confidence is essential to emotional health and courage for living, but Kingdom people must learn to depend exclusively upon God-confidence. This is how they are able to walk in faith regardless of the shifting sands of circumstances.

A common phrase being heard wherever this fresh anointing is moving is to "enter in." But many sincerely ask, "How do I enter in?" Step one to entering into the moves of God is to turn off the voice of your flesh. Refuse to acknowledge the objections of your pride and submit your mind and body to God.

Blessed Are They That Mourn

Blessed are they that mourn: for they shall be comforted (Matt. 5:4 KJV). Jesus said. Blessed are those who examine their innermost being and "mourn" at what they see! After challenging His followers to look inside themselves at their abject poverty of righteousness, Jesus tells them to mourn over the spiritual skeletons in their lives. The self-righteous, religion-satisfied Pharisees were, in Jesus' words, *full of dead men's bones.* Educated on religious logic, they were starved of the Word of God. *Don't boast in your knowledge,* Jesus warned, *but mourn at your poverty of true spirituality. Then you will be comforted.* Paul echoes the same refrain in his letter to the church of Corinth:

> For even if I made you sorry with my letter, I do not regret it; though I did regret it. For I perceive that the same epistle made you sorry, though only for a while. Now I rejoice, not that you were made sorry, but that your sorrow led to repentance. For you were made sorry in a godly manner, that you might suffer loss from us in nothing. For godly sorrow produces repentance to salvation, not to be regretted; but the sorrow of the world produces death (2 Cor. 7:8-10 NKJV).

No person can walk in the joy of forgiveness who has not first come through the tunnel of repentance. Paul said that *the sorrow of the world produces death.* But look at what Godly sorrow works in us!

> For observe this very thing, that you sorrowed in a godly manner: What diligence it produced in you, what clearing of yourselves, what indignation, what fear, what vehement desire, what zeal, what vindication! In all things you proved yourselves to be clear in this matter (2 Cor. 7:11 NKJV).

Acknowledging our sins in the light of God's Word burns

away bondages many of us are not even aware of having. One of the most frequent testimonies to come out of this present revival is a new "feeling of liberty." The lethargy is broken and the door of the cage is opened.

Godly mourning now begins to make sense. Jesus' hard words now look more like a surgeon's scalpel. In spiritual terms, it is called "the fire of God." Fire cleanses, liberates, and sets free those who are held captive to all sorts of bondages. And the "fire of the Holy Spirit" is always an accompanying feature of any great move. It clears the record between us and God. It melts the anger between us and our fellow human beings.

A family I know only vaguely dropped in on one of our "fresh anointing" services. Their young son came forward for personal ministry. As Pastor Paul laid hands on him in prayer, the Holy Spirit showed me a struggle going on in his heart with his father. In a word picture I saw a fence with a gate. On either side were links in the fence. The young boy stood at one link, his father at the other. Then these words flowed out of me: "Your father has a life and calling of his own. You also have your own life and calling to fulfill. However, you must stand in line with your father and go in at the same gate he uses. There is order in God's system. Yet, it is possible to be obedient to your father and still come into your own work. This is God's way, and walking with God will make it possible."

Following this, the father and son joined each other at the altar. There God gave us the Word, *Restoration! Restoration! Restoration!* Following this pronouncement, four men and their teenage sons came and stood before the altar for prayer. It was one of the most touching moves we have seen of the restoration work of this present outpouring of the Spirit.

The hearts of the fathers are being turned to their sons, and the sons to their fathers, as Malachi prophesied. But before there can be this kind of healing restoration, fires that are more than capable of burning the binding ropes must be allowed to kindle in our hearts until every bondage goes up in smoke!

Blessed Are the Meek

Blessed are the meek: for they shall inherit the earth (Matt. 5:5 KJV). The word meek as used here is the Greek word *praus* which refers to man's relationship to man as well as to God. In this statement Jesus is speaking of relationship which means "close connection." Kingdom citizens are called to a "close connection" with God and God's people. Jesus said the meek shall inherit the restored earth as their rightful inheritance, because they have become in their "will and desire" the same as God wills and desires in everything.

Only the meek, those who seek God's will and God's glory in a situation, can overcome the present supernatural violence that has been loosed upon the earth. The one who has determined to give all honor and glory to God will never seek position or personal gain. This worldly rivalry and jealousy is what Paul feared for his new converts at Corinth:

> For I fear lest, when I come, I shall not find you such as I wish, and that I shall be found by you such as you do not wish; lest there be contentions, jealousies, outbursts of wrath, selfish ambitions, backbitings, whisperings, conceits, tumults (2 Cor. 12:20 NKJV).

This was also the point of Jesus' exhortation when He said:

> ...You know that the rulers of the Gentiles lord it over them, and those who are great exercise authority over them. Yet it shall not be so among you; but whoever desires to become great among you, let him be your servant. And whoever desires to be first among you, let him be your slave—just as the Son of Man did not come to be served, but to serve, and to give His life a ransom for many (Matt. 20:25-29 NKJV).

Ungodly competition that drives men to commit crimes and society to sanction the crimes is not the attitude of the meek. The meek follow the example of their Master who loved enough to reach out with all He had—including His life. Yet, He never begged one person to accept what He offered, nor compromised one principle in order to ensure His position among men. The blessing of the meek is not recognition, but relationship—genuine, sound relationship based on solid, Godly principles.

This fresh anointing of God is causing the Church to be meek, to surrender, to put people before things and to put Jesus before all. Meekness without God at its core becomes weakness with compromise at its core. Godly meekness gives strength for tough living.

One morning during a time of worship a very quiet man from a reserved Orthodox background suddenly burst into tears and laughter. It was like an arrow shot into the atmosphere of our service. The Holy Spirit suddenly began to move over the entire place and people received numerous touches from God. After the service was over, the gentleman who had burst out in a tearful laughter confided that he had no intention of doing so, and in fact had been rather skeptical of this new phenomenon in our church. "But I have been so burdened about my business, talking with my lawyer, going over in my mind what to do with tenants who refuse to pay their bills, that suddenly, I was just able to release it all to God!" That is Godly meekness, seeking to be rightly related to God and man.

The confusion of language in Babylon came out of a broken relationship with God. Since that time, communication breakdown has been an underlying plague in every generation. The blessing Jesus promised the meek was restored relationships—the ability to listen, hear, understand, and refocus. Our church has embraced and shared more with each other in the past few months than in all our previous years combined. Our crust of pride and self-awareness is being melted away by a genuine meek caring.

Blessed Are Those Who Hunger and Thirst for Righteousness

Blessed are they which hunger and thirst after righteousness: for they shall be filled (Matt. 5:6 KJV). With greater clarity, this could be translated, "Blessed are they who crave righteousness—they shall be filled with righteousness." Intense longing for right standing with God and man is promised to those who have assessed their spiritual poverty and found their solution lies only in being filled with God. The question is: How do we get filled with God?

The Book of Acts talks of men and women being "filled with the Spirit." Like today's gas tank in a busy automobile, the Church was exhorted to continually be filled with spiritual fuel from the Holy Spirit. Jesus was expressing, in this beatitude, a kind of hunger and thirst that is a continual craving that will cause us to deny ourselves one thing in order to make room for another.

Hunger is the natural signal that it is time to replenish an empty space that normally should be filled. Craving implies the presence of a stronger need—a need sometimes resulting from a deficiency that can impair the health of the organism if it is not met. Hungrily, the true believer anticipates whatever experience the Father will supply, even if it is painful, because his craving for God must be met.

For whatever reason, I once experienced a severe craving for several months that only one single food seemed to satisfy. When I woke up in the morning, the first thing to hit my mind was my craving. Breakfast at the most exclusive restaurant in Boston could not have tempted me in the least. Flaky Danish, piping hot breads, fresh butter, sizzling meat, cheeses or eggs—none of these stood a chance beside my craving for a simple, exclusive brand of wheat cereal, which fortunately happened to be quite healthy. What was even more amazing was that it was a cereal I never cared for before. It was a craving that didn't make any natural sense.

We do not "naturally" crave the good, healthy things of

118

God, either. He supernaturally places a craving for himself within us. Those who have a truly spiritual craving to seek after God, after His Word, after righteousness, may rest assured God has given it to them. When you have an inward spiritual gnawing that refuses to go away, pay attention to it! Such cravings are initiated by God.

Another truth I learned from my "healthy cereal craving" was the error Christians often make when they are attempting to conquer some problem in their life. Phobias, addictions, relationship problems—these and many other natural cares (or pleasures) often become the focus of a believer's life. In an effort to conquer the very thing that troubles us, we tend to focus exclusively on it. We talk it, we think it, we live it.

In reality, a person who will focus in on God, get busy with God's business, immerse himself in God's work—talk, think and live God—will starve his or her problem to death. During my period of craving I never once had to struggle against temptation to eat some "problem" food. I simply was not tempted by any delectable goodies that were not good for me—I wanted my cereal! My craving controlled my eating patterns which ruled out any wrong foods.

True craving eliminates all other competition. Temptations, bribes, payoffs, etc., are usually powerless to change the mind and will of a person with a craving. Ask someone addicted to drugs or smoking or alcohol or gambling and see if you can tempt him or her to quit for a sum of money, a new suit, or a gold watch. Never! Once that craving begins to roar, he or she would rather satisfy it than to own a city. So it is with those who hunger (crave) and thirst after righteousness, those who find nothing satisfies like God.

Where do you find the cravers in the Church? Wherever God is pouring out His Spirit! With joy they are drawing water out of the wells of salvation and they are drinking from the new wave of revival washing in from heaven.

A scene has just flashed across my mind's eye as I sit here in my office. I remember the closing service of a recent revival where people of at least fifteen different nationalities, races and cultures, were laughing, crying, embracing and enjoying the Presence of the Lord and each other. They were entering in with tremendous liberty and self-abandonment so that the cravings of their souls might be satisfied. May the Lord continue to bring about this craving in His people. The Church has contented itself with a "minimum daily requirement" of spiritual existence long enough!

Blessed Are the Merciful

Blessed are the merciful: for they shall obtain mercy (Matt. 5:7 KJV). As the end of this age draws near, the merciless hatred, violence and greed of the human nature is bursting into full bloom the same way the evening sun looms biggest at sunset. Our daily newspapers and evening newscasts confirm this for us every day. Recently, one such story told of a young, drug-using mother in Boston who took her three year-old child's hands and as punishment boiled them in scalding water until the skin fell from the bones. The condition of the human race in the last days before the coming of Jesus is described as selfishness in full array:

> For men will be lovers of themselves, lovers of money, boasters, proud, blasphemers, disobedient to parents, unthankful, unholy, unloving, unforgiving, slanderers, without self-control, brutal, despisers of good, traitors, headstrong, haughty, lovers of pleasure rather than lovers of God... (2 Tim. 3:2-4 NKJV).

We have come to a point of time where the world is never going to settle down and become decent once again. The fruit of the knowledge of "good and evil" has spread worldwide. Not until Jesus comes and expunges sin from the earth will creation be healed of its plagues.

I recently overheard a conversation between an international and an American. "This country is not what I expected," the foreign visitor said. "I don't want to stay in

America permanently. It's too violent." I have news for that disillusioned visitor. Wherever he goes, he will experience the same, for violence, immorality and ungodly arrogance are the mortar of today's world system. This mortar has cracked under the divine shaking begun across the face of the earth, and its toxicity is leaking out into every facet of society. Broken marriages, immorality, violence and lawlessness are touching every nation.

When technology hit the market back in the 1950s, Bibles were thrown into the deepest closets. Those who were experiencing a social sense of guilt over the changes in America breathed a collective sigh of relief when the scholars, the humanists and the media announced to one and all: "God is dead." The whole world became overnight worshipers of the mind and the "things" that satisfy physical lusts. "If it works, do it. If it sells, supply it. If you want it, take it." Mercy found no place and no welcome in this philosophy.

Without Godly influence, man is unmerciful. He is hard and uncaring about the welfare of another. Mercy in the Greek, *eleymon,* means divine sensitivity, tenderness toward one another in view of God. An ungodly society is unmerciful and finds no mercy for itself. It produces courts which will not convict, a government that will not lead, homes that do not build strong families and churches with no power.

During an anointing of laughter in a morning service, one woman took the hand of a woman she hated. "All my hatred melted. It just disappeared," she later confessed. Today's hatred cannot be restrained or redirected into anything constructive by man's understanding. The anger and the hatred rampant in our nation can only be melted by the fire that God is kindling in the Church. It is the only solution that will work. It takes a work of the Holy Spirit to change a heart. Counseling will not do it, resolve will not do it. Human effort may change our mind, but the heart is the territory of the Spirit.

Blessed Are the Pure in Heart

Blessed are the pure in heart, for they shall see God (Matt. 5:8). Society, with its many expressions of intellectualism, Eastern religion and feel-good nonsense, talks about man ultimately achieving a non-violent world that would solve all problems. But violence is simply one form of selfishness.

The problem lies in the hearts of men. When Jesus said, *Blessed are the pure in heart,* He was referring to those who have recognized the bankruptcy of the human nature without supernatural influence. This is a guilty generation. One reason today's world cannot bring itself to convict the guilty is because society is bent on denying the existence of guilt. Other people's sin makes a sinner feel better. In America we like to say that a person is innocent until proven guilty. This is not actually true. A person is guilty if he has violated the laws of man or God, whether or not he is ever found guilty. Guilt and purity are based on what God sees, not what man thinks to be right or wrong.

The compromised say, "Let us do evil that good may come of it." In other words, the end justifies the means. The pressure to compromise is one of the most subtle temptations of the Christian walk. It is the single greatest cause of spiritual weakness and ineffectiveness in the Church's long history.

Compromise is the result of worshiping an impure "God" of our own making, in place of the unchanging Sovereign God of eternity. The world is filled with descriptions of God, everything from carved objects to the man upstairs with the big stick to His being nonexistent. Sadly, too often the Church also seems unable to focus on the real truth of His character and His purposes.

The program of God's Kingdom has always been an unbroken series of fresh moves of the Spirit. Yet, whenever a new supernatural, divine movement appears, the Church's historical reaction has always been to pull the reins tight and yell, "Whoa! We need to analyze this. No swimming or submerging allowed until we have ascertained that the water is actually holy."

This response generally happens prior to and sometimes totally outside of any seeking of God in earnest prayer for revelation and direction. Man's immediate "knee-jerk" reaction does not occur because proof exists that truth is being violated—it generally occurs because traditions would have to be abandoned if truth were to validate a fresh anointing.

As Israel cringed at Jesus' ministry, the Church cringes at His Spirit's ministry in our day. And the Church dislikes being in the posture of "cringing." We are hard pressed to make drastic changes in our secure, if stale, little worlds. *Blessed are the pure in heart,* Jesus said. But without a fresh stream of anointing flowing into and out through us, purity and freshness are impossible to maintain.

I once did a special television program about Charles Finney, the agnostic lawyer who met Jesus and became a great evangelist. But all the material I could find presented Finney as an evangelical in the traditional sense, with no hint of supernatural manifestations. Yet, Finney had numerous "Pentecostal" experiences. For example, he once went into a factory during working hours and everyone became so intoxicated in the Spirit, he had to leave. On another occasion, God directed him to go to a dance hall in upper state New York. "Lord, I don't dance," he responded.

"Go anyway," the Holy Spirit said. Finney reluctantly went to the dance hall where a woman came up and invited him to dance. "Go" the Spirit nudged.

Finney went out on the dance floor and said loudly, "Wait!" Shocked, the band stopped playing. "Before I do anything, I always pray," and then he bowed his head, closed his eyes and began to pray. Soon he heard the sound of a thud! Thud! Thud! The patrons of the dance hall fell out under the power of the Holy Spirit and ended the evening. In that same town, it is on record that not one arrest was made for six months after a visit from Charles Finney.

When fresh moves of the Spirit come, God ceases to show himself in former, usual ways and shows himself in new ways. For instance, when Pentecost came, God ceased showing himself in the Temple. Those who insist upon trying to place God's behavior in a box will gradually slip into a powerless ministry, regardless how many followers they have in agreement with them. There will be churches today where God will cease showing himself powerfully if they refuse to flow with His signs and manifestations.

Blessed Are the Peacemakers

Blessed are the peacemakers: for they shall be called the children of God (Matt. 5:9). This is true now, as well as in the future Kingdom age. Children of the King are expected to refrain from "dog fights" in the flesh.

When Jesus said, *Blessed are the peacemakers,* He was challenging the spirit within human nature that exalts and aggressively pursues self-interests without thought of consequence—spiritually, morally or socially. *Follow* (pursue, chase, seek after, follow closely) *peace with all men.* Jesus said. In other words, make no room for personal revenge or cruelty, even against your enemies.

Pastor Bill Ligon and his wife D.J. were in Guadalajara, Mexico, teaching in a Bible school. The two of them had only recently entered into this fresh anointing, and they had no idea what to expect as they ministered in their church's mission outreach. Bill decided to introduce the students to the revival. He taught them that the anointing is for all people, not simply the clergy, and as he spoke the anointing fell on the students. Spiritual manifestations of signs and wonders began to occur in the classroom.

The next day, one young man whose family had continually fought with him over his enrollment in the Bible school had this report:

I went home and the fighting with me began again. I asked my family to please gather around the table and let me explain what had happened. As I was talking to my family, all four of them fell out under the power of God and onto the floor. When they got up, the fight was over. (Later reports from this young man confirms that although his family was not converted, the fighting has ceased.)

This is the power of the Holy Spirit which is more than able to overcome strong opposition, even in our own families. Jesus is the Prince of peace and with Him, nothing can stand in opposition.

Blessed Are Those Who Are Persecuted

Blessed are they which are persecuted [pursued, harassed, hunted] *for righteousness' sake: for theirs is the kingdom of heaven* (Matt. 5:10 KJV). On the heels of every revival in Church history have come the "hunters," those who seek to discredit fresh anointings and genuine changes in the hearts of changed people.

A well-known Christian writer and public figure was quoted in Charisma magazine as saying the Charismatic move was a failure. Certainly some people failed who were in the spiritual stream that men have named "Charismatic." But to say any spiritual outpouring, any fresh move of the Holy Spirit has failed is an arrogant assumption.

Speaking from a purely subjective point of view, the fresh stream of God that washed over our family in the 1970s has been a blessing that has literally swept thousands into the kingdom of God. That is why we are not hesitating to become immersed all over again in what God is doing in this hour.

According to the beatitudes of Matthew 5,

"Supremely blessed, fortunate and well off are:

1. The poor in spirit—they are the salt of the earth that prevents decay and they will rule the nations in the

Millennium.

2. They that mourn—they will be continually comforted by the spiritual power and glory their lives
   exhibit now and in the age to come.
3. The meek—they inherit what they need now and vast
   wealth in the age to come.
4. Those who hunger and thirst for righteousness—they
   will be filled with great works and achievements.
5. The merciful—they live in the continual mercies of
   God each moment.
6. The pure in heart—they see right from wrong now.
   They will see the face of God in the age to come.
7. The peacemakers—they shall be called the "children
   of God." In eternity this will be the most desirable
   reputation of all creation.
8. The persecuted—they will have great rewards and
   honor among the famed prophets of the living God,
   but probably not in this age."

Any person who desires to stay aflame with the zeal of
God must flow with the Spirit of God, allowing God to work
within him as well as through him—all the way to the end.

Appendix

An Interview with Bill Ligon

Pastor Bill Ligon served as a Southern Baptist Pastor and foreign missionary for eighteen years before founding the Christian Renewal Church of Brunswick, GA in 1973. Since that time, the ministry has grown into a fellowship of thirty churches and one-hundred-twenty five ministers and missionaries.

He is a graduate of Carson Newmar College and holds a Master of Divinity degree from the Southern Baptist Theological Seminary. He has done additional graduate work at Oral Roberts University. He is the author of Discipleship, the Jesus View *and* Imparting the Blessing to Your Children.

He and his wife Dorothy Jean reside on St. Simons Island (Georgia) and have two sons.

Mona: Bill, in your messages I hear you using terms such as "fresh anointing, a visitation, revival." What exactly do you mean?

Bill: For some time now, many pastors in this country and others have been experiencing a spiritual lull. My congregation and I were asleep. The first thing I did after I entered in to this fresh anointing was to apologize to my congregation for not allowing Jesus to do whatever He desires in our worship services. Until revival came to my church, I had a fixed program and period of time which I had allotted to God. He had to work then or He could not work at all.

The Holy Spirit is being poured out upon the Church in a fresh anointing. He wants to be in charge. We are in the beginning stages of a revival that is being conducted by the Holy Spirit.

Mona: How do you compare this present visitation to the Charismatic Renewal of the 1970s and 80s?

Bill: This visitation will be much larger. The Charismatic outpouring was sent to revive the Church, to immerse or baptize them in God's power. This fresh anointing is being sent to equip the saints to go out and get the job done, with signs and wonders.

Mona: An explosive phrase—signs and wonders. Could you elaborate on signs and wonders as they relate to the Church today?

Bill: A sign is any tangible manifestation of the Holy Spirit. As I was speaking in a Bible school in Mexico recently, the power of God fell and the students became drunk on the Spirit of God. I instructed the students that the purpose for this manifestation was to equip them to go out and minister in the marketplace of life. The next morning one student, who never had any experience of praying for others, related the following incident:

> I was going home yesterday when I saw a crowd of people in front of the bank. As I walked nearer someone said, "A man is having a heart attack. They have called for an ambulance."
> At that moment, the Holy Spirit spoke to me and said,

"Go lay hands on the man and command the heart attack to leave." I argued with the Lord, reminding Him that I had never done anything like this and I certainly didn't want my first experience to be in a crowd of people. Three times the Spirit urged me to lay hands on the man. Finally I walked over and obeyed the Lord.

As I prayed the man began to vomit. He got up, shook himself and said, "I feel fine!" Then he walked away and into the crowd. I couldn't believe God would use me like that!

From the beginning, God announced His intention to give signs of himself to man. Genesis 1:14 quotes God saying of creation, *Let there be light...let them be for signs....* Israel was delivered from Egypt with signs and wonders. Isaiah prophesied of Messiah and his followers: *...I and the children whom the Lord has given me are for signs and wonders...* (Isa. 8:18 KJV). This is clearly Jesus and the Church. Jesus himself spoke of *signs of the times* (Matt. 16:3). He performed signs and wonders throughout the Gospels, and He declared that *these signs shall follow them that believe* (Mark 16:17).

Signs should be a very normal part of the Church's ministry. Every believer has the anointing within himself or herself for signs and wonders. That is one purpose for this fresh visitation. God is stirring up the anointing in His people that will enable them to give evidence to the fact of Christ.

Mona: You use the phrase "drunk in the Spirit." What exactly do you mean by this term?

Bill: Mona, I posed this question to God, "Why are you getting people drunk in the Spirit?" And this was what He responded: *I have to get My people drunk in My Spirit because they have been drunk on the world. Their minds have been polluted, they feed their doubts—there is no confidence in Me and My power. I have to get them so drunk that I can change their thoughts and their attitudes.*

Mona: Could you give us another example on a benefit from someone becoming drunk in the Spirit?

Bill: Two examples come to mind that give real insight into spiritual intoxication. One was a husband who became drunk in the Spirit in a service where I was ministering. The next day when the man returned to services, he related a story of a failing marriage. "I just didn't love my wife any more," he said. "She couldn't do anything to please me. While I was out in the Spirit, God showed me that I had a critical spirit and He delivered me of it."

A second example is an eight-year-old boy who fell out in the Spirit and was spiritually drunk for more them an hour. When he became sober, we asked him what had happened. "Angels came and jumped on a trampoline with me. Then Jesus spoke and told me to obey my parents and study hard." As the young boy started out of the service, the power of God fell on him again and he lay in the hallway for another hour. Acts 2:41 gives a good example of what happens when people become spiritually intoxicated. On the day of Pentecost, one hundred twenty Spirit-drunk believers went out into the street and the Church grew that day to well over three thousand. Spiritual intoxication allows the Holy Spirit to impart spiritual instruction. Life-changing experiences occur where people fall under the power of the Holy Spirit.

Mona: Again you have introduced a problem term for some people. Why do people "fall under the power of the Holy Spirit?" Is this really necessary?

Bill: Standing requires a certain amount of motor control. Conscious control of the body is active when we are standing and operating under our own power. Releasing the body to the control of the Spirit yields all strength to God and allows us to put our whole attention on God.

While in a meeting with a well-known international leader who was experiencing this new anointing, I asked him how this fresh anointing was being transferred. This was when my wife and I were still investigating it. He replied, *Sit under the anointing in meetings with reputable preachers where it is manifesting, and don't resist the power of God.*

After that, my wife and I have submitted at every opportunity. Sometimes we get so drunk in the Spirit we slide out of our chairs. But we don't resist Him. Occasionally, we will just get up and lie down as an act of surrender and allow the Holy Spirit to minister to us.

Mona: Bill, there is a "sign" in this present visitation that is really a challenge for many. It's the laughing. How can we justify all this laughing that is present in many of the services? Is laughing really from the Holy Spirit?

Bill: You know it is amazing how much reverence for the devil I have discovered since this fresh anointing. God's people have an unholy fear of the devil. They honestly believe that hundreds of believers can come together in the name of Jesus, worship and sing unto Him, pray and preach His word—only to have the devil come in and take over the service with a mocking laughter.

God, not Satan, is omnipotent. Do we honestly believe that Satan can come into the house of God and take over a service that is being conducted to His glory? The only demons that can come into a worship service are those that people personally bring in with them. And they won't stay long when the anointing comes.

We need to shake off this unholy fear of Satan. He is not greater than God. There is a mocking laughter and there is a holy laughter as your book explains. Great restoration and release are occurring as God's people are entering into holy laughter.

Mona: Many have been praying for revival. If this is the answer, what can stop this revival?

131

Bill: So far as I see in Scripture, nothing but religious or cultural tradition can hinder the flow of God's Spirit. No man can stop God, but we can hinder the flow of His Spirit, especially in our personal lives and in the lives of those under our influence.

Mona: Where do we go from here?

Bill: Preparing the way for the Lord. Evangelism. I believe God wants churches to grow, not from members moving from one church to another, but with spiritually new-born people out of the world. A pastor in Mexico came to our church for a series of meetings to sit under this fresh anointing. Within two months, his church has doubled in size.

In any visitation, the Lord is always seeking the lost, but revival begins in the house of God. Before God can bring the lost into the Church, He needs a revived family in which to place the new-born believers. Revival in the church is a signal that a harvest is coming in the world.

Mona: You say the anointing has come to "equip the saints." Were not we equipped when we were born again?

Bill: John 20:22 says that Jesus breathed on His disciples and said, *Receive ye the Holy Ghost.* At that point the Holy Spirit came into the disciples and the new birth took place.

In Luke 24:49, Jesus instructed His disciples to wait for the promise when He would send the Holy Spirit upon them. This is when the Baptism of the Holy Spirit took place.

In John 7:38, Jesus said of those who believed on Him, *Out of his belly shall flow rivers of living water.* The outflowing of the Holy Spirit took place when the anointing came upon the disciples.

So we see here three different works of the Holy Spirit within the life of the believer. The Spirit comes "in" to us for the new birth. The Spirit comes "upon" us for the baptism of the Holy Spirit. The Spirit come "out" of us under the anointing for spiritual works.